CW01636352

BE

A DIRECT AND SIMPLE APPROACH TO EMOTIONAL REGULATION, BE-ING CALM, UNDERSTANDING YOURSELF AND SELF-COACHING THROUGH ANY SITUATION, SO YOU CAN

NOLAN COLLINS

RAMP

CONTENTS

First Edition 2024

ISBN: 978-1-7396670-7-8- (PAPERBACK)

DISCLAIMER

The information contained within this book or my website is not a substitute for professional advice such as from a medical doctor, psychiatrist, or counsellor. The information provided does not constitute legal or professional advice, nor is it intended to be.

Diagnosing psychological or medical conditions is for trained medical professionals (physicians and therapists).

Any decisions you make and the consequences thereof are your own. Under no circumstances can you hold Nolan Collins or RAMPIT Solutions Ltd liable for your actions.

This book is dedicated to you, the reader, the person who wants to be the change.
You are the reason I write. Thank you for giving me a purpose that gives me such joy, passion and desire to be better.
You are worth it.
I also dedicate this book to my daughter, Nia, who has always accepted my apologies, understands I will always be a protective dad, gives me many opportunities to practise my skills of be-ing, and is my best friend. You make my heart smile every day.

FOREWORD

> …the supreme goal of all theory is to make the irreducible basic elements as simple and as few as possible without having to surrender the adequate representation of a single datum of experience.
>
> ALBERT EINSTEIN

In other words, "keep it simple."

I'll try.

If you want to let go of the thoughts, emotions, behaviour and reactions that stop you from being happy, calm and in flow, there are four elements that have to be balanced: Our sense of safety, our perception of gain or loss, how clear we are about what's happening (or not) and a healthy sense of self.

Sounds simple, right? Let me put this in context.

When you find bliss, quiet, inner peace, or that slippery and seemingly elusive state of being "at one" with yourself, you have a sense of being safe, being connected to yourself, being clear about who and where you are and have that feeling of being good about yourself and where you are mentally and emotionally. You are neither affected by nor affecting the world around you.

When you feel this flow, you don't question it, because everything seems to make sense.

Be-ing is the state of allowing yourself to react to nothing, with purpose.

Unfortunately, we don't find or stay in that state very often because life happens. Kids, work, partners, hobbies, the pets, the car, other people, and we start losing ourselves. We start being affected, emotional and reactive because we think we need to react, respond, fix or figure out, and we don't know how to process every situation to keep us in that desired bliss state, yet.

We start losing that clarity, finding ourselves in defensive positions and feeling a need to prove ourselves, tell others what they're doing wrong and "to" us, and often find people who, through a lack of self-awareness, seem to rob us of our joy.

When we lack clarity or any of the BE elements are disrupted, we question everything, including ourselves, our parents, the past and every situation that didn't go to plan.

That is who I ended up being—a man lacking clarity of purpose, self-awareness, responsibility, and any semblance of emotional regulation. I used my full 6'5" frame to prove my point when I knew I was "right" and felt as if I had to know all the answers all the time. I hated my behaviour and would berate myself with "that's not me" under my breath when I know I was being affected, and the affector, in an unhelpful way. Yet the only person who heard it was me.

After having to shut down a business several years ago I struggled mentally and emotionally. It was a big hit in many ways. We lost our house, cars, friends, income, self-respect, drive, and motivation to try again. I had some pretty dark thoughts, and it was the love I had for my kids that kept me pushing forward.

I didn't want to believe my business wouldn't work and as my life fell apart, so did I. I had always landed on my feet and managed to make things work. This time it didn't, and I didn't know why or how to behave when it all came crashing down.

I had forgotten how to "be".

We ended up moving to Florida, then back to England.

I took a training job, teaching digital marketing to apprentices, and found joy in training again. That is my passion: seeing the light go on when students have that insight that brings things together. My best jobs always involved teaching or training, from restaurants to ballroom dancing, massage therapy to sales and digital marketing.

I spent many hours coaching my students on more than marketing. Many were lost, confused and doing the apprenticeship as a last resort. More than a few broke down in tears, wondering how they ended up there. I could relate!

It was through teaching these young adults that I created a framework for dealing with shifts and change and helping them figure out what was missing or unpolished to get them back on track. That is the RAMPIT Framework I talk about later. Within that framework, I identified four key elements that affect our emotions, state, reactions, responses, triggers, and resulting behaviour: the BE Elements.

Together, the two frameworks are influential whether the outcome is positive and helpful or negative and unhelpful.

When I started really understanding the importance of these BE elements, everything changed. I understood where my emotions were coming from, ***and*** my triggers ***and*** my reactive behaviour. Importantly, I learned how to stop reacting and just be.

It was like a huge weight was lifted from my shoulders, allowing me to see and think clearly for the first time in years.

My relationship with my children, which had worsened with the Covid lockdown, dramatically improved and is now stronger than ever.

I got divorced and met someone who helped me put all of this into practise and had the strength to see the real me, and allow that Nolan to not only appear, but stay and become the person I am today.

My son recently sent me a WhatsApp message that reminded me what a monster I used to be.

He told me he'd found an old video of him crying in his room, with me yelling in the background.

After I told him I was truly sorry, he told me it was okay. He said we've come a long way since then.

And he told me he loves me.

Yes, I cried. That meant so much to me. It still gets me when I read this again!

When I changed, he changed. We have a great connection now that I never thought I'd get back.

He accepts me for who I am today and has also learned to be present and focus in the present. He also understands why he behaved the way he did and knows how to be less reactive now.

So does my daughter, and she had to live with me during lockdown! My son was smart enough to live with friends!

I was about as far from being emotionally regulated as you could imagine only a few years ago. Knowing what I do now, and what you're about to learn changed my life.

I'm not perfect by any means, however, I know how to catch myself when I feel myself going off the rails. I know how to stop and break old patterns, habits and behaviours that don't serve me or help the situation. And I know how to reflect on myself so I can be the change and be the person who benefits my relationships, *my* life and my clients.

And this is why we're here.

"Be" is a book that explains how the four simple root elements affect all our reactionary situational emotions, triggers, and reactions. Good and bad. Helpful and unhelpful. These four elements affect our ability to be happy, successful, loved, present, mindful, purposeful, calm, deal with the past, the present and moderate those anxious thoughts of what might be, what hasn't happened, and more.

They lie dormant in our subconscious until shift, change, or what we're not expecting knocks us sideways, and they try to take control. You'll learn how pitting them against perceptions of how we are told to react can help you find peace in the present.

You'll also understand yourself and others when tensions rise, expectations aren't met, and even when everything is flowing in perfect harmony.

More importantly, you will learn how understanding the BE Elements and playing to their strengths can ***help you let go of unhelpful situational emotions and find calm, emotional regulation, and a level of self-control and self-confidence in almost any setting that you likely have not experienced before.***

What does this mean in plain English? It allows you to not get angry, or "feel you have the right" or "need" to have reactive emotions. That is your brain telling you clearly that you don't know how to process the situation, your bliss has been disrupted and force you to defend your position. Even if that defence is only in *your* head.

Every situation is neutral until you put meaning to it.

This is not about becoming robotic, emotionally detached, emotionally repressed or pushing your feelings down until you explode—far from it. It's about knowing which emotions to trust and embrace and which to dissipate through seeking answers and solutions.

When you understand why things are flowing, you can really experience those highs of positive and helpful emotions on a much deeper level, and fully lean into them.

It is also a practical guide to knowing what to do when you recognise these elements and want to address them so you can be more responsive, less reactive and "be".

"I would have written a shorter letter, but I did not have the time"
Blaise Pascal

As you read this book, you'll want to overcomplicate it and add to it, and tell me there is something missing and there's something I haven't included. You'll be right. I can't fit every scenario in here any more than a driving instructor can predict every situation you'll come across for the next 50 years on all the roads in all the cars you'll ever drive in the few lessons you take to get your license. Yet you'll get a piece of paper saying you're ready to tackle the dangers of the road, knowing you'll be forever learning and adapting. Yet we don't get anything like that for driving our lives. Until now.

Understanding the BE Elements means understanding them well enough to be able to adapt to situations as they come up.

If you asked me to teach you to drive, I'd tell you to understand what the accelerator, clutch, brakes and steering wheel do. You can go a long way with those 4 things.

So too will you be able to with the four BE Elements (and the other stuff I include here for good measure!)

My goal here is to keep things as simple as possible. Life and understanding ourselves has become so complicated it's almost impossible to even see the basics anymore. Just as a new driver needs to learn the accelerator, the brakes, the gears, the clutch and steering, so too will going back to basics help you accelerate your happiness and clarity. Pun intended! This is not Formula 1, and like most situations we are faced with on a daily basis, needing a Formula 1 steering wheel with all the buttons and controls to drive to the shops can just overcomplicate things.

As you continue your journey through this book, you'll realise that any closed, limiting or restrictive thoughts can be explained in this book. It will all make sense by the end and you'll either be upset at how simple it is and how you've been overcomplicating things for so long, or you'll accept it and learn to just… be.

You'll also realise which of the four elements, and where you sit on the spectrum for each one are causing you to react, behave uncharacteristically, and be able to ask yourself self-reflective questions to come to terms with it, and get past it.

If you want to reach self-actualisation and even transcendence, read this book all the way through and discover how these four elements affect our present moments and thoughts and our representation of the past.

Strip away labels such as masculine and feminine and their stereotypes, avoidant, attachment styles, narcissistic tendencies, inner child, and any other psychological label that tries to define who you are, have learned to be, or use to justify your learned behaviour. This is going to be hard for a lot of people as we are bombarded with labels defining who we are and expect our partner, boss, and relatives to understand it all.

Remove other people and their actions and external influences **and discover who you were in those difficult situations** and which of the four elements were affecting you and possibly other people. It makes dealing with the past much easier. It allows you to be whoever you want to be. It allows easier access to the open state of being happier, in love, calm, tolerant, understanding, empathetic, creative, purposeful, accepting, aware, open, receiving, inviting, and giving.

Unless, of course, you really ***want*** to be closed, reactive, emotional, avoidant, unhappy, egotistical or malicious. No? I didn't think so.

Here's what I'd like for you to accomplish by the end of this book:

- I'd like you to feel happiness on a higher level more frequently and be fully present with it.
- I'd like you to look at the shifts and setbacks you encounter as neutral situations that you know you can deal with because you'll know how to "be" when things aren't going to plan.
- I want you to never lose sense of your worth, no matter how much, like a paper £100 note, it gets abused or yelled at, or trodden on. You will always be worth so much, and more.
- I also want you to be able to let go of the past and understand that other people's actions are based on where they are (or were) on the spectrum of the BE elements, and there is nothing you can do now to change that. ***You*** can choose to BE the person ***you*** want to be now.

So, if you're ready to "be" the change, "be" all you can be and just… "BE", read on.

With heartfelt love (I finally get it), Nolan

INTRODUCTION: THE ART OF BEING

Every single day, we're bombarded with demands for our time and attention; the art of "being" has never been more essential. This book is an exploration, an invitation, and a guide to understanding the undercurrents of our emotional lives through a simple yet transformative perspective that challenges the very foundations of how we interpret our feelings, thoughts, emotions, triggers, and reactions.

I'm not here to teach you how to blame a situation that caused you to be who you are or lay blame on someone from the past. We're going further in before we can navigate the "now" and learning how your understanding, awareness and relationship with your state of be-ing in past situations, and how not knowing, understanding or being adept in those states has both impacted you, *and can be undone, so you can be fully present now*.

We are predictive creatures by nature. Our minds continuously forecast, plan, and anticipate. But life, as we all well know, is the master of surprise. When the unexpected occurs, our emotional equilibrium is often the first casualty. Emotions run high, reactions overtake responses, and clarity becomes clouded by confusion. But what if we could anticipate these emotional ebbs and flows? What if we could understand the root "whys" behind our emotions with such awareness that we remain composed and in control no matter what is happening around us?

"BE" is not just a book; it's a journey toward becoming the person who understands this and lives less reactively, chooses to respond and is able to respond with calm, clarity and confidence in yourself. It's about embracing the unpredictable nature of life while maintaining an unshakable inner calm, even in strange or unfamiliar situations. It's about letting go of the shackles of our past and living in the present with a clear focus on how to manage the future.

The benefits? They're profound and plentiful: increased emotional intelligence, heightened self-awareness, better decision-making, more effective self-coaching, stronger relationships, and an undeniable sense of presence in every moment of your life.

Conversely, the implications of not mastering this skill are equally significant. Without the ability to self-regulate our emotions, we're at the mercy of every shift in our environment, every word spoken in haste, and every internal dialogue that leans toward the negative. It's the difference between being at the helm of your ship or being the dinghy tied to the back, being tossed about by the cruel, unending sea of our past, battered by the immovable rocks of our environment (and the people around us!).

This book is crafted for you — the professional striving for balance, the parent seeking harmony at home, the individual yearning for a measure of peace amidst the chaos. It's for those who wish to dive deep into the mechanics of their emotional life and emerge with a blueprint for serenity.

Here, you will discover expanded chapters that delve into the very reasons why the four BE Elements — a sense of safety or not, gain or loss, clarity or confusion, and a sense of Self vs Ego — are present in our lives and how to navigate them when they serve us least. Each chapter is a stepping stone toward recognising where we are, what we're feeling, why we're feeling it, and how we can shift our perspective to one that serves us — and those around us — much better.

By the end of this book, "BE-ing" will take on new meaning. It will be less about doing and more about understanding, less about reacting and more about responding and engaging with life in a manner that is both enlightened and enlightening.

So, embark on this journey with an open mind and a willing heart. Discover the transformation that awaits when you learn to simply... BE.

One last thing, and this is really important. I am not here to tell you how to deal with unhelpful behaviours, your partner, kids or coworkers, or tell you not to be emotional, or try to replace one emotion with another. Neither you nor I can change other people. You ***can*** influence them through your actions, responses and behaviour. We also can't change the past or even often address it because there are too many contributing factors that made those past situations a part of who you are today.

This book is a way to be, now, so you don't fall into those reactive, retaliatory unhelpful behaviours or have emotional outbursts. I want you to stop ***expecting*** that you'll have a reaction and be able to look at every challenging shift or situation in a neutral way and ***choose*** how to proceed. You already know how to do this in many situations, just not the ones that don't make sense, yet. Don't worry, I'll show you how to do that too.

THE END

"Begin with the end in mind" – Dr Stephen Covey.

I think that's a good start so let me tell you what the end looks like.

BE-ing can mean different things to different people, so I'll do my best to explain what I think it can include and the goal of this book.

BE-ing is letting go of other people's expectations

BE-ing is finding calm through knowing how to ride the storm

BE-ing is accepting others, whatever their intention and knowing they are still learning

BE-ing is allowing unhelpful words and events to flow through you and not get stuck in you

BE-ing is finding what makes you happy

BE-ing is living in the moment without thinking about be-ing!!

BE-ing is fostering a safe environment for yourself and others.

BE-ing is being present with yourself despite your past

BE-ing is modelling the BE Elements in every relationship unconsciously

BE-ing is knowing there is a solution

BE-ing is choosing to do what is helpful for yourself and others

BE-ing is freeing yourself of the clutter of unhelpful thoughts and emotions

BE-ing ***is asking questions, and being prepared for the answer you don't want to hear, and being ok with it!***

BE-ing is adding to the situation, even when sometimes that means being silent.

BE-ing is remembering that every situation is neutral until we put meaning to it.

BE-ing is being able to acknowledge the past, but not let it stop, limit or restrict you today.

BE-ing is embracing the four BE Elements to find love, joy and happiness for yourself and others.

BE-ing is understanding you can only change yourself and, by doing so, can influence others.

Be-ing is remembering that just because someone else is reactive, you don't have to join in!

BE-ing is acceptance: Accepting you will never fully understand the people around you. Accepting they want to be better and often don't know how. Accepting that we are all doing this for the first time and will make mistakes.

BE-ing is the ultimate emotional regulation. When you can learn to simply be, you have learned to regulate whatever comes your way.

NOTE: Regulating emotions is not dismissing or ignoring them. It is understanding them and being able to choose a response that helps you, first and foremost.

Everything I talk about in this, and my other books is focused on helping you BE the person you want to be, and letting go of the person you think you need to be for others. If they are the same, that's great, however most of the time it's not.

Look at that list above of what Be-ing entails. Imagine living like that. How would that feel? Calm? Freeing? I know it may seem unrealistic, or I'm trying to sell tickets to fairyland. I'm not. This is possible. I know. I live it every day, despite my past.

If you're already thinking "I bet it wasn't that bad", you could be right. To some people, comparatively, it wasn't. Yet it could be worse than others. I am a male statistic in many ways; however, I choose not to let my past affect my present. It uses way too much energy!

ARE YOU READY FOR THE SHORTCUT ALREADY?

I'm going to share, right here at the front of the book, the short version of this simple process of breaking the patterns of triggers and reactions, preparing your for those times you know you're going to get emotional, or manage to break away from the drama to get your head back on.

The secret to being calm and non-reactive is to understand the factors that contribute to not being. When you learn to acknowledge, accept, anticipate and align with those factors, being gets easier.

It is not just one thing because the solution is never the same in every situation. As you go through the process below, take time to assess where you are, where you're struggling, where you need help, and where you can help, in each situation you feel something is not aligned and causing you to react.

All of this may not make sense yet. That is what the rest of the book is for; however, knowing where you want to be will help what you learn to be more contextual.

STOP – Understand your past – stop the reaction

- **Say: THAT JUST HAPPENED / THIS IS HAPPENING**
- **Remember: THERE'S A REASON FOR THAT**
- **Ask: WHAT IS MY INSTINCTIVE REACTION / EMOTION?**
- **Question: DOES IT NEED TO BE? (DO I WANT IT TO BE?)**

BE – **Be present**

- **HOW AM I BE-ING RIGHT NOW?**
- **WHERE AM I ON THE SPECTRUM: SAFETY, CONNECTION, CLARITY, SENSE OF SELF?**
- **HOW ARE THE ELEMENTS AFFECTING ME / AM I LETTING THEM AFFECT ME?**

RAMP-IT – **Prepare for the future**

- **WHAT'S THE DESIRED OUTCOME AND WHY?**
- **WHO AM I BEING / DO I NEED TO BE?**
- **HOW DO I / WANT TO FEEL?**
- **WHICH EMOTIONS ARE HAPPENING (AND WHY?)**
- **WHAT CAN I DO RIGHT NOW?**
- **WHAT/WHO DO I NEED TO DO IT?**
- **IS IT HELPFUL?**

WHAT CAN I LEARN FROM THIS?

HOW CAN *__I__* BE PREPARED IF/WHEN THIS HAPPENS AGAIN?

There is a printable cheat sheet at https://nolancollins.com/bebookresources

Now you know what BE-ing looks like, and have a simple process for coaching yourself through a situation, let's move on. By the way, this works for planning and growing when life is flowing too. It's not just for identifying what to work on when things are going wrong! Seriously. Go back through the shortcut phrases above for something that's going well, and you'll see!

It's 2024 and I'd be silly not to include some online bonus material or a way to get more help, join a community so you can ask questions and more. You can find all of that at https://nolancollins.com/bebookresources

IMPORTANT NOTE:

There is a big difference between accepting other people for who they are when their intentions are good yet aren't clear on how to process or explain their own emotions and tolerating intentional, unhelpful or malicious behaviour. Most people are in the first category as we are not taught how to communicate when we don't understand a situation. Recognising YOUR emotions and reactions come from YOU not understanding an aspect, or having clarity, is YOUR first step to not reacting when someone else is! Taking things personally is a **you** issue, and is often the cause of the exacerbation of simple misunderstandings!

When you can self-regulate it also gives you the power to know when to step away from what is not helping you.

There are times when emotions are necessary, and time is needed to process them. Loss and grief are included there. My goal here is not to diminish or invalidate any emotions; it is to help you be aware when emotions become the go-to response and limit you from being when there is an underlying state that can be explored, understood and processed first.

Most people do not have malicious intent. Not your kids, or your in-laws, or your partner. Even when then it seems they do, it is still their reaction and you still have a choice in whether to receive it internally or not.

Remember that.

PART ONE

CHAPTER 0 - START HERE

WHO IS THIS BOOK FOR?

"BE" is crafted for the seeker in each of us—the individuals standing at the crossroads of growth, looking for a signpost that points toward deeper understanding and fulfilment. It's for those who find themselves pondering the questions of who they are, what they want, and how they can navigate the complexities of life with a sense of purpose and peace.

You might be a professional striving to balance ambition with inner peace, a parent wishing to cultivate a nurturing and understanding environment for your family, or a student navigating the waters of self-discovery and academic pressures. You could be someone at a transitional point in life, questioning your next steps and seeking a foundation of clarity and confidence on which to build your future.

No matter your specific journey, if you're looking for a guide to help you understand the nuances of your emotions, triggers, behaviours and reactions and how these elements shape your reality, this book is for you.

HOW TO USE THIS BOOK:

"BE" is more than a collection of insights—it's a practical guide designed to be actively used in your daily life. Here's how you can make the most of it:

Reflective Reading: Approach each chapter not just as a reader, but as an active participant. Use the sections as mirrors, reflecting on how each aspect of the BE Elements and The Experience Loop is present in different areas of your life.

Exercises and practises: At the end of each chapter, you'll find exercises designed to deepen your understanding and application of the concepts discussed. Dedicate time to these practises, approaching them with openness and curiosity.

Journaling: Keep a journal as your companion through this journey. Use it to document insights, emotions, and revelations as you navigate the book. Journaling is a powerful tool for self-reflection and consolidation of learning. If journaling is not for you, send yourself voice notes, or just sit and be with the content and take time to reflect on it.

Discussion and Sharing: If possible, share your journey with others. Discussing your insights and experiences can enrich your understanding and provide new perspectives. Consider joining or forming a study group with fellow readers. If you're part of the Self Coach Community, you can join others there discussing it, and I can join in. If you are in a relationship, please do this together. Even teenagers understand what is in here!! There will be an audiobook version soon after the book is published.

Integration into Daily Life: Look for opportunities to apply the BE Elements in your daily interactions, decisions, and reflections. The true essence of this book lies in its application beyond the page—into the fabric of your daily life.

Repeat and Revisit: "BE" is designed to be revisited as you grow and evolve. Your understanding and application of the BE Elements will deepen over time, offering new insights with each reading.

I'll state the obvious and let you know that there is a level of repetition in this book for a few important reasons:

First, some people will jump to chapters they think they need to work on. I call this flat tyre syndrome. You see a flat tyre and assume the cause is where it is flat. I advise against dong this, but it's your time so do what you want!

Also, many of the tips, suggestions, exercises, and questions are relevant in different contexts, so they bear mentioning again in the context of the chapter.

We all take in information in different ways. I may say the same thing a couple of different ways. If you're thinking "you just said that Nolan", that's a good thing that you registered it, understood it and recognised the different version. The next question I'd ask is this: Are you applying it?

A NOTE ABOUT THE LACK OF EXAMPLES OF "WHAT TO DO WHEN..."

As you'll discover in this book, and most of my others, I tend not to give examples of scenarios and how to react in those situations.

The reason for this is that there are too many contributing factors to the situation, from all sides. You only know yourself, and often don't realise why you are reacting to a situation, so to tell you to react a certain way when most of us don't know ourselves, and certainly don't know exactly what someone else has been through, their intent, or understanding of you is tantamount to placing a thousand land mines in front of you, blind folding you and say go for a walk, you'll be ok!

Use what is in this to learn how not to be reactive. Learn how to be responsive. Learn how to understand yourself and model the behaviour you want to see in and from others. Even when it's hard. Especially when it's hard.

Use what's in here to learn how to "be"!

CHAPTER 1 - HOW TO STOP OVERANALYSING AND ENJOY THE FLOW OF BE-ING

In mastering emotional regulation and self-coaching in relationships, many people struggle with overanalysing their actions, emotions, and interactions. This is a natural and normal part of learning when developing any new skills. It can also hinder our ability to be present and enjoy the flow of BE-ing when we forget to lean into the situations we've been working on and trust ourselves to simply be.

Understanding the stages of skill acquisition can help us navigate this process more smoothly and realise that the initial overthinking is how we process new skills, until we don't have to.

Why do I keep using the word "skill"? It's because personal development, self-coaching, and improving emotional regulation are all skills you can develop when you know the basics and apply them consistently.

If you're learning to bake a cake there's a good chance the first few attempts will be a labour of love, sweat and tears, hopefully not in the cake! Over time it gets easier, you remember the ingredients and the order to add them. You tweak the baking based on new ingredients, your oven and the size of the cake.

You stop getting frustrated when it doesn't turn out exactly the way you want and a way to work with it.

Eventually it becomes automatic, and you can even help someone else when they are starting out and see where they are over thinking and making simple mistakes.

We go through four stages of competence, explained below, when learning any skill, from driving, to dancing, to cooking, to hard skills and soft skills in the workplace. Here they are broken down in context.

THE FOUR STAGES OF SKILL ACQUISITION IN EMOTIONAL REGULATION

Unconscious Incompetence: In this initial stage, we are unaware of our deficiencies in emotional regulation. We may not recognise how our actions and reactions impact ourselves and others, or we might not yet see the potential for change. This lack of awareness can lead to unintentional harm in relationships and hinder personal growth.

Conscious Incompetence: As we start to explore self-coaching and reflect on our behaviours, we become acutely aware of our emotional regulation gaps. This stage often brings discomfort and frustration as we recognise what is unhelpful and struggle to correct it. It's a critical phase where awareness begins, laying the foundation for change.

Conscious Competence: Through deliberate practise and self-coaching, we start developing the skills needed for better emotional regulation. We must consciously think about our actions, decisions, and responses, particularly in challenging situations. This stage involves actively managing our emotions and being mindful of our reactions, fostering a more controlled and deliberate approach to interactions.

Unconscious Competence: Eventually, with consistent practise, these skills become second nature. We navigate our emotions and interactions with greater ease and fluidity, responding to life's challenges calmly and constructively. This stage embodies the essence of "being"—living with a sense of inner calm and resilience, allowing us to handle difficult situations with grace and composure.

Most of us operate within the middle two stages—conscious incompetence and conscious competence—especially when mastering complex skills like emotional regulation. It's crucial to understand that overthinking and meticulous analysis are part of the learning process to start and it's ok. You can't just jump to unconscious competence because you want to any more than driving became automatic after your first lesson. Although this stage can feel overwhelming, it's a necessary step toward achieving unconscious competence, where emotional regulation becomes an effortless and natural part of our lives.

THE PREDICTIVE NATURE OF HUMANS

Did you know that as humans, we're part of an exclusive club? It's called the Predictive Club. Yes, our brains are hardwired to forecast and expect outcomes based on past experiences and patterns. This isn't about weather predictions or guessing the end of a movie. It's about how we navigate our everyday lives, anticipating the future at every turn. You'll learn more about this with the Catalyst Stack later in the book.

The Double-Edged Sword of Anticipation

But here's the twist—our predictive powers come with a catch. They can sometimes trick us into expecting more troubles than triumphs. Ever found yourself worrying about a presentation at work or imagining worst-case scenarios for a new project? That's our predictive nature focusing on potential problems, not solutions. This tendency, while useful in some cases, can lead us to feel overwhelmed, anxious, and stressed.

Shift the Focus

Anticipating solutions rather than problems not only helps us manage our stress but also improves our overall approach to life's challenges. By embracing a more anticipatory style, we can enhance our emotional resilience and open ourselves up to a world of possibilities.

Remember, the goal here isn't to ignore potential risks or problems—it's about balancing our view and responses so that we're not just reactive but also proactive and responsive.

I invite you to reflect on your own predictive habits. How often do you find yourself anticipating the negative? Can you shift that to start expecting the positive more often? Try the exercises we talked about and see what changes for you.

WHEN THINGS DON'T GO AS PLANNED: TRIGGERS, TRAUMA, EMOTIONAL REACTIONS AND LEARNED BEHAVIOUR.

You know how sometimes the smallest things can just set you off? It could be a word, a look, or even a memory that sends you into a tailspin of emotions. Ever wonder why? Well, it's not just about what's happening right now; our reactions are often echoes of our past experiences, and our inability to process it then the way know how to today.

Why Do We React the Way We Do?

Our emotional responses, whether they're the knee-jerk reactions or the deep-seated fears, stem from the blueprint of our past experiences. Every situation we've navigated, from childhood to now, has left a mark on how we interpret and react to the world around us. If as a kid, you were thrown into situations you felt unprepared for, those moments didn't just disappear; they shaped your understanding of how safe or threatened you feel when new challenges pop up as well as how safe it is to ask for clarity.

"Who you are and how you perceive everything is based on your ability or inability to process every situation that you've experienced

up to this moment, and you're understanding of the BE Elements and RAMP Factors." Nolan Collins

For instance, if your early environment felt like a minefield—where making mistakes meant trouble—you might find yourself overly cautious or defensive today. It's like your mind set up a defence system that says, "Better safe than sorry," whenever anything remotely challenging comes up.

UNDERSTANDING TRAUMA AS A RESPONSE TO THE UNEXPECTED

Trauma can often result from situations that catch us completely off-guard, where we don't just feel unprepared—we are overwhelmed and unable to cope. It's essential to recognise that trauma isn't just about the big, obviously terrifying events. It can also stem from an accumulation of smaller stresses that feel just as overwhelming without the right tools or support.

Being sensitive to this, acknowledgecrucial that trauma affects everyone differently. Some may experience trauma from events that might seem less extreme but were personally significant due to their history, the environment, the intensity or timing. This does not make their experiences any less impactful or challenging.

Trauma can create deep marks in our emotional fabric, often altering how we perceive safety and risk. Understanding this can help us approach our own traumas and those of others with the compassion and empathy needed to move forward.

I'll repeat what I've already said above as it applies to trauma as much as any other situation.

"Who you are and how you perceive everything is based on your ability or inability to process every situation that you've experienced up to this moment, and you're understanding of the BE Elements and RAMP Factors."

Your trauma, labels, wounded child, avoidant, narcissistic, ghosting, and unhelpful emotional responses to everyday situations are the remnants of not knowing how to, or being able to process situations in the past as they happened or in the present. Once you know and remember that you are not still living that moment, and you have a way to live purposefully today, they stop limiting you and in most cases, stop being traumatic.

I'm not saying the memory of those incidents will disappear; however, how you relate to them can and will change—IF you want it to.

I guarantee there is at least one situation you've been in when someone else is freaking out, overwhelmed or breaking down and you're thinking to yourself "it's not *that* bad".

You think it's not bad because your experience has given you the tools to process that situation differently than the person who can't. At that moment, anything you say to try to help is going to seem absurd, unrealistic, and unattainable, yet you know it is all true and there ***is*** a way to handle the situation differently.

In those situations, try to remember a situation where you felt out of control until you discovered the solution and were able to process the situation and not be affected by the same thing happening again. Be the person who asks if they'd like help finding a solution. And, if you're the type of person who wants to say, "it's not that bad", try offering help and guidance instead of berating someone for not having lived your experiences!

We are not taught what you're about to learn as children. We do not know how to process words, behaviour, emotions, or other people's actions. We take it at face value until it affects our state of being, and we don't know how to explain it or deal with it, so our reaction and response becomes a learned, reactive and often emotional behavioural response.

You may be offended or caught off guard by my blunt approach to this; however, if you want to "be," then you will learn to lean into the hard, challenging, and often blunt truths and embrace them, despite not understanding or accepting, yet, that it ***is*** possible to simply "let go." Most people who have overcome trauma state that they just stopped letting it affect them and decided to move on. They learned to "be" and focus on the now. You'll learn that part when we come to the RAMP-IT framework.

THE RIPPLE EFFECT OF EMOTIONAL REGULATION (OR THE LACK THEREOF)

When we struggle with emotional regulation, the effects can permeate various aspects of our lives, often in subtle yet significant ways:

Lack of Emotional Regulation:

Unpreparedness: We may fail to anticipate challenges or obstacles, often because we're fixated on past experiences or operating on autopilot, hoping for the best. This lack of foresight can lead to unnecessary stress and crises.

Normalisation of Stress: Signs of stress are often dismissed as "just another day," leading to the normalisation of harmful patterns that, over time, can disrupt our well-being and relationships.

Cognitive Overload: Our brains, in an attempt to protect us, may go into overdrive, obsessively analysing discrepancies between reality and our expectations. This mental overload can cause anxiety, confusion, and decision-making paralysis until we regain clarity and reassurance.

Ripple Effect When Emotionally Regulated:

Proactive Preparation: With emotional regulation, we become more adept at anticipating and preparing for potential challenges. This foresight allows for a more measured and thoughtful response, reducing the likelihood of being blindsided by unexpected events.

Healthy Stress Management: Recognising and addressing stress early helps prevent the normalisation of unhealthy patterns. This awareness fosters a more balanced lifestyle and enhances our capacity to manage life's pressures healthily.

Mental Clarity and Stability: Emotional regulation brings a sense of calm and clarity, reducing cognitive overload. This balance allows us to navigate discrepancies between expectations and reality more smoothly, promoting resilience and adaptability.

By understanding and managing our emotional responses, we can create positive ripple effects that enhance our overall quality of life, fostering healthier relationships and a more resilient mindset. Conversely, neglecting emotional regulation can perpetuate cycles of stress and confusion, making it harder to achieve a sense of stability and well-being.

A MORE HELPFUL WAY TO HANDLE LIFE'S SURPRISES

Let's swap out the old defensive playbook for something a bit more proactive. Think about an emergency responder—a firefighter, let's say. When a call comes in, they don't panic; they respond with precision. They've trained for chaos, learned to anticipate various scenarios, and know what tools to use. Their preparation and understanding allow them to manage real and anticipated danger and act effectively. This is called managed fear. It's still scary to be in that situation as it's not all in your control; however, knowing how you can handle it, if you must, OR walk away if that's the best option, gives you back some control.

We can approach our emotional challenges with the same level of expertise and preparedness. By understanding our triggers and the reasons behind our reactions, we can train ourselves to handle emotional fires more adeptly:

- **Recognise the triggers:** Identify what sets you off and why. Is it a tone of voice, a type of situation, or a particular time of day?

- **Prepare your toolkit:** Develop strategies that help you deal with triggers. This could be deep breathing, a quick walk, or a mantra that brings you back to centre.
- **Respond, don't react:** Give yourself a moment to choose how you want to respond rather than letting old patterns dictate your actions.
- **Read this book** and reflect on which of the BE elements felt out of alignment or unclear when the original event happened or is happening.

By taking control of our responses and understanding the root of our emotions, we can transform our lives from reactive to proactive. We can't change the past, but we can definitely reshape our present and future. Let's start handling life's curves not just with survival in mind, but with a strategy to thrive.

THE POWER OF BEING LESS REACTIVE, AT PEACE AND SELF-AWARE

It's easy to get swept up in a whirlwind of reactions. Whether it's a stressful email, an unexpected bill, or even just a spilled coffee, our default mode can too often be one of tension and reactivity. But imagine for a moment if we could change that default setting. Imagine the peace and clarity that comes from being less reactive, more at peace, and deeply self-aware. It's not just calming; it's empowering.

Here is a simple phrase to get you started. Say this in the mornings before you interact with anyone else. "Whatever happens, I can handle it. Whatever happens, I'm good." And then have a process of what to do or think to get through it (the shortcut earlier in the book can help!)

WHY REACTIVITY CAN HOLD US BACK

Reactivity is often our first line of defence against unexpected challenges. It's quick, it's automatic, and it's usually charged with emotion. While this can be useful in genuine emergencies, in everyday scenarios, this kind of knee-jerk reaction can lead us to make decisions that aren't in our best interest in the long run. We might snap at a loved one, make hasty business decisions, or retreat into bad habits, all because we're in the grip of reactivity. And this reactivity stems from one of the four BE elements being out of balance.

SELF-AWARENESS AS A PATH TO EMPOWERMENT

Self-awareness is about knowing yourself so well that external circumstances lose their power to destabilise you. It means understanding your triggers, your concerns, and your habitual responses so intimately that you can choose to act differently. This level of self-awareness is profoundly empowering. It not only allows you to navigate life's challenges with more grace but also opens a space for peace and contentment to flourish, no matter what's happening around you.

By embracing the power of being less reactive and more at peace, you don't just change how you respond to the world; you change your entire experience of life. It's a journey well worth taking, filled with insights, growth, and a deepening sense of calm that will serve you in every area of your life.

BENEFITS OF EMOTIONAL REGULATION AND PRESENCE

Emotional regulation and being fully present are not just skills; they're transformative practises that enhance every facet of your life. When you master these abilities, you not only improve your own mental and emotional health but also enrich your interactions with others and your overall experience of life. Here's a closer look at the benefits that come from honing these powerful skills.

Enhanced Quality of Life

Increased Resilience: Emotional regulation helps you bounce back from setbacks and challenges with greater ease. By managing your emotions effectively, you're less likely to be overwhelmed by negative feelings and more likely to adopt a proactive approach to problem-solving. This resilience opens a smoother path through life's ups and downs, allowing you to recover more quickly and thoroughly.

Clearer Thinking: When you're present and emotionally balanced, your capacity for clear thinking and concentration improves. Emotional turmoil can cloud judgment and lead to impulsive decisions. In contrast, emotional regulation provides a clear mental space for making informed decisions, allowing you to weigh options objectively and foresee potential outcomes more accurately.

Improved Relationships

Deeper Connections: Emotional regulation and presence enhance your relationships. By understanding and managing your emotions, you reduce the chances of miscommunications and conflicts. Being present also means you're truly attentive when interacting with others, which fosters deeper, more meaningful connections. This attentiveness shows your care and respect, making others feel valued and understood.

Enhanced Empathy: The ability to regulate your own emotions is closely linked to empathy, which is the capacity to understand and share the feelings of another. When you're in control of your emotions and fully present, you're better equipped to perceive others' emotional states. This understanding can lead to stronger, more empathetic responses, fostering compassion and closeness.

Personal Growth and Development

Greater Self-Knowledge: Regular practise of emotional regulation and mindfulness increases self-awareness. You become more attuned to the nuances of your thoughts and feelings, which can lead to insightful revelations about your personal needs, desires, and areas for growth. This self-knowledge is invaluable for personal development and setting meaningful life goals.

Reduced Stress and Anxiety: One of the most immediate benefits of emotional regulation and being present is a significant reduction in stress and anxiety. By focusing on the current moment and managing emotional responses, you minimise the impact of stressors and prevent anxiety from taking hold. This not only improves your mood and energy levels but also has long-term health benefits, reducing the risk of stress-related illnesses.

Boosted Performance and Achievement

Improved Productivity: Presence and emotional control directly impact your productivity. When you're not sidelined by emotional reactivity or overwhelmed by wandering thoughts, you can direct your full attention to the task at hand. This focus maximises efficiency and effectiveness, whether you're at work, studying, or pursuing a hobby.

Heightened Creativity: Emotional regulation can enhance creativity. By maintaining emotional balance, you create a conducive environment for creative thoughts to flourish. Being present helps you notice details and make connections you might otherwise miss, fuelling innovative thinking and creative problem-solving.

Embracing the practises of emotional regulation and presence transforms not just how you feel day-to-day but fundamentally enriches your approach to life. These skills empower you to navigate both personal and professional challenges with grace, enhance your relationships, and unlock your full potential in various aspects of life. Engaging with the world from a place of balanced emotion and mindful presence is perhaps one of the most profound changes you can make for a fulfilling and harmonious life.

RETHINKING FEAR: UNDERSTANDING EMOTIONS BEYOND SIMPLE LABELS

You've probably heard it a million times—every limitation, every hesitation is rooted in fear. But let's take a moment to unpack that. It's not always as black and white as many coaches or self-help gurus might have you believe. Emotions, reactions, limitations—they're complex, and boiling them all down to fear oversimplifies the vast spectrum of human feelings.

The Spectrum of Being

When we talk about emotions, we often use terms like 'fear' as a catch-all, but what we're really dealing with is a whole range of experiences, each sitting somewhere on a spectrum. At one end, yes, there's fear. But it's not the whole story. Every emotion we feel, from doubt to elation, has its nuances, and recognising this can give us a clearer, more empowered understanding of our inner world.

The Myth of Fear

Think about the last time you hesitated before a big decision or felt nervous about a new opportunity. Was it really fear, or something else? Labelling these moments as fear can trigger unnecessary emotional responses. It's like being told you're scared every time you pause to think, which isn't just inaccurate—it's unhelpful. This approach can lock us into a state of anxiety, making us feel like we're always battling our own nature.

Understanding the True Roots of Our Emotions

Here's where the BE Elements come into play. These elements—a sense of Safety, Gain/Loss, Clarity/Confusion, and Self/Ego (yes, I'm going to repeat them many times in the book so you both remember them and also don't get frustrated having to look for the page where I explained the four elements earlier in the book!)—help us understand what's really at the heart of our reactions. Instead of jumping to 'I'm scared,' we might find we're feeling uncertain because we lack a certain piece of information (Clarity), or perhaps we're worried about potential loss (Gain/Loss).

Seeing Beyond Fear

It's time we move beyond the fear label. By recognising the real roots of our emotions, we can address them more effectively. Are you truly afraid of success, or are you concerned about the added responsibilities it might bring (Gain/Loss)? Are you afraid of commitment, or is it about losing your sense of independence (Self/Ego)?

Practical Steps Forward

Next time you find yourself labelled with fear, pause and ask yourself:

- What BE Element might be influencing this feeling or apprehension?
- Is this reaction truly about fear, or is it about something I need more clarity on?
- How can understanding this help me move forward more confidently?

Reserve Fear for When It's Really Fear

Fear has its place. It's a vital emotion that can protect us from danger. But when we use it as a blanket term for every challenge or setback, we reduce its significance and potentially miss out on understanding our true motivations and needs. Let's keep fear in its rightful place and use the BE Elements as our guide to navigate the complex landscape of our emotions. This way, we aren't just reacting to life; we're engaging with it meaningfully, with clarity and purpose.

As we dive deeper into the BE Elements, I'll guide you through common scenarios often mislabelled as fear and show you how to reassess and respond to them with new understanding and less anxiety. This isn't about coping; it's about thriving by truly understanding and embracing the complexity of our emotions.

One last thing here. The next time you or someone else uses fear as an excuse for not doing something, try rephrasing your concern without using the word fear. Get specific and see what comes up for you.

CHAPTER 2- IS IT HELPFUL?

MY MANTRA FOR EVERY THOUGHT AND ACTION WE TAKE.

When it comes to opinions, thoughts, actions, feelings, and emotions, slapping on a label of 'right' or 'wrong' just doesn't sit right with me and often leads to defensiveness as one of you now feels "less than". It's all subjective, isn't it? Think about the end of a relationship—it might not look great from the outside, but sometimes, it's the healthiest move for everyone involved. Each person gets a fresh start. Sure, it's tough, but with the right self-coaching, you can come out stronger on the other side. I talk more about this in one of my RAMPIT RUNDOWN books and trust me, I've been through it myself. Twice.

Of course, I get that there are extreme cases where right and wrong are clear cut, especially when it comes to the law or situations of life and death. But for most of us, thankfully, those aren't everyday occurrences.

That's why in my coaching and my books, I talk about what's helpful rather than what you 'should' or 'must' do. It's not for me to say my viewpoint is more important than your own experiences, your values, or your needs. I'm only human, so I might slip up now and then—feel free to nudge me back on track if I do!

In the online community I've built, the first rule is to share what's worked for you personally and avoid telling anyone what they 'must', 'should', or 'have to' do.

As you read through this book, or any of my work, there's just one question I encourage you to keep in mind: Is it helpful?

If it isn't, what's the alternative?

Figure out what helps you in the here and now. That might shift over time, and that's perfectly fine. When things change, learn to flow with that change, and discover what's helpful in your new context.

KEEP IT SIMPLE, SUNSHINE: SIMPLIFYING SELF-HELP AND PERSONAL GROWTH

It's no secret that the world of self-help and personal growth can sometimes feel overwhelmingly complex. But does it really have to be? Think about it like learning to drive—it's all about mastering the basics first. When you're driving, you know the essentials: speed, gear, direction, and timing. You adjust these based on the road conditions and traffic, seamlessly integrating these basics without much thought once you're experienced.

Back to Basics with BE and RAMP-IT

The same principle applies to navigating life using the BE elements and the RAMP-IT framework, which I get into a bit later. These tools are like your life's steering wheel, brakes, and accelerator. They help you handle the twists and turns, accelerate when you need to move forward, and slow down when you need to take in the scenery or make careful choices. By understanding these basic tools—like knowing when you're acting out of a perceived or real lack of safety (a BE element) or need to prepare better for future challenges (RAMP-IT's Anticipate step)—you can manage life's challenges more effectively.

Why Complicate Things?

Just as you wouldn't hop into a Formula 1 car without knowing how to handle a regular car, you shouldn't overwhelm yourself with advanced personal growth tactics without nailing down the basics. We often excel in some areas of our lives, like our careers, while we might struggle in others, such as personal relationships or managing stress. That's because we're trying to operate in fifth gear in one area, while we're barely out of first in another!

Driving Your Life with Confidence

By going back to the basics, you can build your confidence and comfort level across all areas of life. It's about syncing up those gears —aligning your BE elements with your actions and using RAMP-IT principles to map out a smoother route. This approach doesn't just simplify personal growth; it demystifies it, making it more accessible and manageable, just like driving your favourite route with ease.

So, let's reduce the complications. Let's focus on understanding our fundamental reactions and behaviours, using straightforward tools that guide us through life's complexities. By keeping it simple, we enhance our ability to navigate life not just with skill, but with grace and confidence. Remember, every expert was once a beginner, and every pro driver started with turning on the engine and figuring out how to shift gears smoothly. Let's take that approach to personal growth and enjoy the journey, one basic skill at a time.

And make it helpful!

PART TWO
CHAPTER 3 - UNDERSTANDING THE BE ELEMENTS

In my first book There's a Reason For That, I explained a little about the four elements in a more cursory capacity. I included them as part of the mind-body state awareness section, and for those books, they fit in there perfectly.

The goal of this book is to not only expand on these elements but show how they are an important focal point of dealing with triggers, emotions, the past, the present and the future.

The premise here is that when we have an emotional reaction that is either helpful or unhelpful, it is because one or more of the following four root elements are contributing to it.

- A sense of **Safety** – (Mental, emotional and physical) - Think of this as your security system. It's all about feeling snug as a bug, mentally, emotionally, and physically. When it comes to work or relationships, it can also mean financial security. Setting boundaries falls under Safety, just like setting a boundary wall to keep zombies out.

- A sense of **Gain or loss** – (Physical or Mental) - This one's the wallet of emotions. It handles all transactions, whether you're pocketing a win or dealing with a loss, including everything from feeling connected at home or work in relationships, to your material possessions.
- A sense of **Clarity or Confusion** (Knowledge and Understanding) – Do you ever get upset because you don't understand someone else's perspective or why they're doing something (or not doing something)? Or think you know the answers only to change your perspective when you get more details? Yup, that's this one.
- A sense of **Self or Ego** – (Knowing yourself vs proving your worth) - Ah, the big 'E'! This is all about how well you know and value yourself versus how much you're trying to prove your worth and value. Our goal is to have a healthy sense of self: acceptacnce, worth, esteem and confidence and keep the unhealthy side of ego in check.

THEY'RE EVERYWHERE!

These elements aren't just passing through; they're the essential ingredients in every emotional recipe. Every laugh, every tear, and every furrowed brow has a dash of Safety, a sprinkle of Gain/Loss, a pinch of Clarity/Confusion, and a heap of Self/Ego.

I put the elements in a specific order, because I believe that's how we adopt the elements from an early age. We are not born with ego; it is developed through learned behaviour and interaction with others.

As a child, our first reactions are about safety and the needs that come with it. A baby cries to be soothed and feel safe. It cries to be fed so it can survive. At this point and even later formative years, we want to know someone, anyone, has our back.

Fast forward a bit, and we're toddlers grappling with the profound concept of 'mine'. Snatch a toy away, and the world ends; give it back, and it's party time again. This is our first dance with the joys and heartbreaks of gain and loss.

Then comes understanding. Why do you think the one phrase we know we're going to get from kids when they hit a certain awareness level is "why"? They want to know more. Details, reasons, clarity so they can make sense of what we are doing and how they should respond. They say curiosity killed the cat, but what we're looking for is for curiosity to kill confusion. Keep asking those questions!

Last comes a sense of self, and ego. This is best described as telling a child they are stupid because they don't understand something or telling them you don't have time for them, and looking at their face. This affects their sense of self. Reward and encourage a child and see their sense of self grow healthily. Children also develop the ego in relation to other kids. My dad can beat up your dad. My toy is bigger than yours. I'm better than you at…, look what I did! The ego, like an alien who seems to control our minds, has landed and the only thing to ward it off is a healthy sense of self.

As adults, not understanding that we have gone through these phases of elemental development often leads to the result we see: reactive emotions, avoidant or agressive behaviour and an inability to self-regulate. When you understand this is how we interpret the world at a root level, and know how to recognise these four elements, the world and our situations become less scary and more manageable.

IT'S ALL RELATIVE

Here's the kicker: the BE elements operate on a spectrum. They aren't just on or off; they slide up and down like the volume on your smartphone. More of this, less of that—it all depends on what life's throwing your way at any given moment. It's like making an emotional smoothie and adjusting the ingredients until you get it right.

The BE Elements are all on a spectrum, both on a sensory and

practical level, depending on the situation, our interpretation of it, our intent, our beliefs, our history and the desired outcome.

For instance, think about the last time you got a gift you really liked. That joy? That's Gain doing a victory dance. Now, remember that gut-punch feeling when you thought you lost your phone? Yep, that's Loss, dragging you down the emotional spectrum. And knowing you lost your phone because you did something silly, like leave it on a wall next to a waterfall, that's a hit to the self-worth when you blame yourself.

Keep this in mind. Highlight it, write it down somewhere or leave yourself a voice note. Remember that both emotions and the four BE Elements are on a sliding scale depending on the situation.

And... our reactions, emotions and learned beliefs are often triggered from the actions of others who, you guessed it, were acting based on ***their*** relative place on the spectrums of these four elements!

No wonder we all have issues!

MAKING IT ALL MAKE SENSE

Have you ever watched someone react bizarrely over something trivial? Like having a meltdown over a misplaced coffee cup? That's these elements playing puppeteer. And sometimes, the strings get a little tangled.

Let's say you grew up in a household where the motto was "mistakes are disasters." That's going to crank up your Safety and Ego dials every time you're less than perfect. Fast forward to adult you, freaking out over a minor work error—thank your upbringing for that encore performance.

So, What's the Plan?

Understanding these elements isn't simply about getting good vibes; it's about setting the stage for how you interact with the world. It's learning that when things go sideways, maybe you're not just "overreacting." Maybe it's just your BE elements, doing their thing a bit too enthusiastically, and while you sense something is off, you can't quite put your finger on it.

And remember, nobody's perfect. Not even your parents had all the answers (shocker, I know). They were winging it too, armed with their own set of wonky BE dials that they picked up from their parents, who picked theirs up from their parents, who picked it up from… you get the picture! So cut them some slack, and while you're at it, cut yourself some too.

Ask yourself this question: How old were you when your parents started self-coaching? For most of us the answer is "within the last few years" or "never". Keep that in mind because you, by reading this book, are already years ahead of your parents and are creating a better environment for yourself, your relationships and your kids, especially if you share what you're learning with them.

Use the BE Elements™ (Not Be element, as in Beryllium!) to self-coach yourself and be your best self **despite** their actions, behaviour and past, because you can't change the past. And you can't change them (your parents) without them being a part of the solution, willingly. Lead by example, even when they don't get it.

A QUICK DIVE INTO EMOTIONS

Let's take a minute to unpack emotions. We've got the big five — anger, disgust, enjoyment, fear, and sadness, as identified by Paul Ekman. Each of these basic emotions is a gateway to a broader range of feelings, which I promise we'll get into later. But for now, let's keep it simple and focus on these core experiences.

The Spectrum of Emotions

Emotions aren't black and white. They vary greatly depending on context, which can significantly change how we react in different situations. For instance, the emotion of fear can range from slight nervousness to paralysing terror. Understanding this spectrum is key to understanding ourselves. This is one of the reasons I stay away from using fear as a catchall phrase, as often it's a little uncertainty that can be overcome with the right approach.

Context Matters

Consider how different situations trigger different intensities and types of emotions:

Divorce vs. Dropping Ice Cream: Someone asking for a divorce might trigger a complex cocktail of emotions, from fear of loss to a sense of relief, showcasing a spectrum from safety to self-worth. Conversely, dropping an ice cream as a child might seem tragic, triggering intense sadness over a simple loss, but as an adult, you might just laugh it off.

Receiving Gifts: The emotional impact of receiving a gift can also vary. A trinket from a tour guide might not stir much emotion compared to winning your favourite sports car, which could send your excitement through the roof. The context here amplifies the sense of gain involved.

IMAGINING SCENARIOS

Our brains are incredibly adept at simulating scenarios, often triggering emotional reactions just by imagining situations. For example, if I tell you to picture receiving a less valuable gift than the person next to you, you might feel a twinge of jealousy or disappointment — emotions stemming from *perceived* loss and ego - why are they more important than me?

Reflecting on Everyday Interactions

Everyday interactions often reflect underlying emotional dynamics dictated by the BE Elements. Whether it's feeling undervalued in a conversation ("They won't listen to me") or sensing a threat to your stability ("I think he's going to leave me"), recognising these elements at play can help you respond more effectively.

Keeping It Simple

Understanding emotions and their triggers doesn't have to be a complex affair filled with jargon. It's about seeing the simple truths beneath our reactions and learning how to manage them, making life a bit easier to navigate. So, let's continue to break down these concepts together, making them as straightforward and actionable as possible. In the end, simplicity is not just about ease; it's about clarity and effectiveness in our daily lives.

UNDERSTANDING EMOTIONS AND THE BE ELEMENTS

Emotions are a fundamental part of our human experience, influencing our thoughts, behaviours, and interactions. To "just be" and remain present, we need to understand and regulate our emotions effectively. The BE book aims to help us achieve this by grounding our emotional experiences in the four BE elements: Safety, Gain and Loss, Clarity and Confusion, and Self and Ego. Each emotion we experience is rooted in these elements and exists on its own spectrum.

Emotions are complex and multifaceted, shaped by our past experiences, current circumstances, and expectations for the future. They are not inherently negative or positive but are indicators of our internal states and reactions to external stimuli. By understanding the root causes of our emotions through the lens of the BE elements, we can better regulate them, respond more effectively to situations, and ultimately, enhance our ability to stay present.

Let's break down how our learned behaviour, present reality, state of BE-ing, and our predictions and understanding of outcomes all contribute to our emotional experiences. In short, our emotions, while incredibly fast to show themselves, are comprised of the following (this goes for both helpful/positive and unhelpful/negative emotions):

- Our learned behaviour
- Mixed with the present reality
- Combined with our state of BE-ing
- adding how it all affects our ***predicted*** outcome
- and our understanding of the ***actual*** events unfolding
- WITH our ability to process and deal with what is happening in the moment
- Or not.

Our Learned Behaviour

Our emotional responses are deeply influenced by our learned behaviours, which are shaped by past experiences, cultural norms, and early life conditioning. These learned behaviours act as a framework for how we interpret and react to different situations.

Example: If you grew up in an environment where expressing emotions was discouraged, you might have learned to suppress your feelings. This learned behaviour can influence how you respond to emotional triggers as an adult, often resulting in an internal struggle to acknowledge and express your emotions.

Mixed with the Present Reality

The present reality includes the immediate circumstances and context in which we find ourselves. It encompasses the people we interact with, the environments we are in, and the challenges or opportunities we face. Our emotional responses are a reflection of how we perceive and react to these present realities.

Example: If you are in a stressful work environment, your present reality might trigger feelings of anxiety or frustration. Understanding how these feelings relate to your need for safety and clarity can help you navigate the situation more effectively.

Combined with Our State of BE-ing

Our state of BE-ing is our overall emotional and psychological state at any given moment. It is influenced by both our internal and external experiences and is a dynamic reflection of how we are engaging with the world around us.

Example: Feeling a sense of loss after a relationship ends can affect your state of BE-ing, making you more sensitive to other losses and gains. Recognising this can help you be more mindful of your reactions and foster resilience.

Adding How It All Affects Our Predicted Outcome

Our emotions also influence our predictions and expectations for the future. How we anticipate outcomes can shape our emotional responses, either positively or negatively.

Example: If you expect a positive outcome from a job interview, you might feel hopeful and motivated. Conversely, if you anticipate rejection, you might experience anxiety and self-doubt. These emotions are rooted in your need for self-esteem (Self and Ego) and security (Safety).

And Our Understanding of the Actual Outcome

Finally, our understanding of the actual outcomes of events shapes our emotional responses. How we interpret and make sense of what has happened can reinforce or challenge our initial emotional reactions.

Example: If you receive challenging feedback at work, your initial reaction might be defensive (related to Self and Ego). However, upon reflection, you might understand the feedback as an opportunity for growth, shifting your emotions towards acceptance and motivation (related to Gain and Loss and Self).

And Our Ability to Deal with What Is Happening

Our ability to cope with and respond to our emotions and situations is influenced by our emotional regulation skills, support systems, and overall resilience.

Example: If you have strong emotional regulation skills, you can navigate stress and challenges more effectively. This ability helps you maintain a balanced state of BE-ing, regardless of external circumstances.

And It's Not All Negative!!

It's important to recognise that not all emotional experiences are negative. Positive emotions such as joy, love, and contentment are also rooted in the BE elements and contribute to our overall well-being.

Feeling a deep connection with a loved one can bring immense joy and fulfilment. This connection enhances your sense of safety, validates your self-worth, and provides clarity in your relationship while giving the "gain" of connection.

CHAPTER 4 - THE TRIANGLE OF BE-ING

HOW WE BE: ALONE, AFFECTED, AND AFFECTING

YES, I do know how to speak English! On my self-discovery journey, I realised that every interaction has three facets: how we are when we're alone, how we're affected by others, and how we affect others. These facets shape how we respond or react and how others perceive us. Understanding these dynamics can help us navigate our emotional landscapes more effectively.

Our goal is to be "at one" with ourselves, with no conflicting thoughts about ourselves, not being affected negatively by what is out of our control as well as not intentionally negatively affecting others. In this state we are also aware that we are safe, but not focused on it, we are neither losing nor gaining, and ok with it, we are clear on where we are and what we're doing without needing confirmation or to think about it, and we are content with ourselves, without needing to dwell on it. This, I believe, is what Eckhart Tolle is talking about when being in the now and not thinking.

Alone in Our BE-ing: Sometimes, the best company is our own. When we're alone, truly alone, it's just us and our thoughts. No noise, no distractions. Whether you're meditating, journaling, or enjoying a solo activity like motorbiking, these are the moments you get to meet the real "you," undiluted and unedited. In these quiet times, we reflect deeply, understand our true desires, and connect with our innermost selves. However, being alone also means facing our inner critic and coach, and recognising how they influence our thoughts and emotions for self-awareness.

Affected by Others: Most of our waking hours are spent interacting with others—absorbing, reacting, and often overthinking. It's human nature. We're social creatures, after all. These interactions can significantly influence our emotions, thoughts, and behaviours. Whether we're inspired by a mentor's guidance, stressed by workplace demands, or comforted by a friend's support, other people's actions and words profoundly impact our state of BE-ing. For example, someone else's words might trigger a defensive reaction in an argument, impacting our sense of safety and self-worth. An important point to note here is that there is a difference between perceived impact and real impact. Knowing the difference and questioning whether it's real or perceived often comes down to understanding the intention of the other person, AND not reacting, but be-ing even if their intention is unhelpful. **I didn't say this would be easy!!**

Affecting Others: The tricky part is recognising not only that we are influenced by others but also how we influence those around us. Most of the time, we hope we're spreading positivity and support. But sometimes, in trying to protect our own emotional space, we might inadvertently affect others negatively. Recognising when we're the affector in a situation helps us act more mindfully and empathetically. For instance, during an argument, our reactions and words can either escalate the conflict or help de-escalate it by fostering understanding and empathy.

THE CYCLE OF INFLUENCE

In many challenging interactions, we constantly shift between being affected by others and affecting others. This cycle can become particularly evident in conflicts or arguments. Here's how it typically plays out:

- Trigger: An event or statement from someone else triggers an emotional response in us (affected by others).
- Reaction: Our emotional response (anger, hurt, frustration) influences our behaviour and reactions towards others (affecting others).
- Escalation: If our reaction is negative, it can trigger a similar emotional response in the other person, perpetuating a cycle of conflict.

BREAKING THE CYCLE:

To break this cycle, we need to understand and apply the BE elements:

- Safety: Recognise when a situation threatens your sense of safety. practise grounding techniques to maintain a sense of security, even in conflict. For example, take deep breaths or step away for a moment to collect your thoughts.
- Gain and Loss: Identify what you're trying to gain or afraid of losing in the situation. Understanding these motivations can help you address the core issue rather than reacting impulsively. For instance, if you're afraid of losing respect, focus on communicating your perspective calmly and clearly.
- Clarity and Confusion: Seek clarity in communication. Misunderstandings often escalate conflicts. Ask questions to understand the other person's perspective and ensure your own

message is clear. Paraphrase what the other person has said to confirm your understanding.

- Self and Ego: Be aware of how your sense of self and ego influence your reactions. Are you reacting defensively to protect your ego? practise humility and openness and be willing to admit mistakes and learn from them.

Going Back to Alone

Let's circle back to being alone. It's also important to recognise that even when you are alone, you can be both the affector and affected to yourself. Our internal dialogue—the ongoing conversation between our inner coach and inner critic—can significantly impact our emotional state. The goal is to recognise when your coach and critic personas are butting in and remind them that it's okay to make mistakes and you don't need to be upbeat all the time. Self-compassion and mindfulness are key to navigating these internal dynamics.

Example: When battling your own thoughts, such as self-doubt or regret, practise self-compassion. Acknowledge your feelings without judgment and remind yourself that it's okay to feel this way. Use helpful self-talk to counteract negative self-talk and reinforce your sense of self-worth.

Putting It All Together

The Triangle of BE-ing provides a framework for understanding how our internal experiences, external influences, and our impact on others all intertwine. By recognising and balancing these aspects, we can achieve a more harmonious state of BE-ing, better navigate our emotional landscapes, and foster more meaningful connections with ourselves and others.

We can "be" at one with ourselves.

Understanding these dynamics, especially in challenging situations like arguments or internal conflicts, helps us move from being reactive to being responsive. By applying the BE elements, we can break negative cycles, foster positive interactions, and maintain emotional balance.

The Triangle of BE-ing is a powerful tool for self-awareness and emotional regulation. By understanding how we are alone, how we're affected by others, and how we affect others, we can navigate our interactions with more insight and compassion. This understanding is key to just "being" present, regulating our emotions, and developing helpful and strong relationships.

CHAPTER 5 - SAFETY

SAFETY, in its broadest sense, is not merely about physical well-being but also encompasses our emotional and mental states.

UNPACKING SAFETY: A PERSONAL JOURNEY

When I was a small child, I stayed with my dad in southern France. He lived in a tiny village surrounded by hills that felt like mountains. It was isolated and safe. However, my sister and I managed to get lost on a walk one day and ended up faced with a giant wall covered in red and black ants. We were probably 4 and 6 years old, me being the younger one.

We were petrified and not only didn't know where we were, we were also afraid of climbing the wall and being bitten by the ants. I probably cried, not knowing how we'd get home. I didn't want to sleep on the mountain in the dark. I knew what was out there; snakes, scorpions and ants. Lots more ants!

Minutes seemed to stretch into hours until we heard the resonant clang of the village church bell. It was so loud we knew we must be close to the village. We plucked up the courage to climb the wall, jumping down the other side while simultaneously shaking our body and brushing off any ants that had latched onto our sandals and started climbing our legs.

When we looked up, we realised we were at the end of the road leading out of the bottom of the village and could see our dad's house. We were safe again, and as kids shrugged it off. Seeing my dad in his workshop was the icing on the cake. He was safety, and probably had no idea why we were running to him with such excitement!

I went back to that wall several years later and realised not only how small the wall was but also how close we had been to salvation the whole time. While we were not in immediate danger, what we didn't know heightened our perception of being unsafe.

I'm going to add this next story in because it is important, and affected me for years, and affected my children as a parent. I almost didn't add it

My mother hit me. I'm not talking a slap on the butt. I'm talking closed fist, beat me until I couldn't breathe, then hug me and tell me she's sorry and loves me. Kitchen utensils could often be used too. This didn't happen every day; however, it was enough to be engrained as a factor in my childhood and adult behaviour until I learned what's in here!

You think I might have been a bit confused in relationships?

If she was upset, she hit me. If my sister did something, she would find a way to take it out on me. If I did something that reminded her of my father, she would hit me or scream at me. She wasn't like this all day every day, but those moments stuck with me, and my siblings didn't get a fraction of what I did. The last time she hit me was when I was 18, sitting in the car with her near my work. I don't remember what triggered it, but I do remember sitting there and just letting her punch and hit me. I'd got to the point that I knew what was going to happen, and reacting would not change it. I asked if she was done, got out of the car and believe that was a few weeks before I moved to America.

This is not everything about my mother. She has some good qualities too, however this constant need to be right, to not be viewed negatively is something that still limits her ability to let go, communicate effectively and openly and be present. It is a behaviour she developed from her own mother, not understanding herself, or me and not knowing how to process some difficult situations.

In the house, I was frequently treading on eggshells, worried that if I said or did the wrong thing, a punishment would be forthcoming. My behaviour didn't help as I was in trouble a lot, often looking for attention and connection in all the wrong ways. I understand why now!

Being defensive was a pattern created from feeling like I was always under attack. It took me years to get over this, and I still get triggered from time to time. However, I know what's happening now, so I swiftly end it. Or my partner does, by reminding me that her intention is not to challenge me but to gain clarity. And she does it calmly, which helps me come back to being able to access my thinking brain and use it, most of the time. I'm only human and have to work on be-ing too!

Just a quick note here. There is no such thing as being perfect. Knowing what's in here doesn't mean I won't or don't slip up or that you or your partner / child won't either. We are all a work in progress. What matters is knowing how to self-regulate when you can, being prepared for those moments of uncertainty, being aware when you find yourself reacting, and being able to reflect on your behaviour openly without first trying to justify it. Just keep doing it, and it gets easier. I promise.

My mother doesn't affect me now because I know why she behaved the way she did, and I get to choose who I want to be. I am safe, both in myself and my environment. Phew!

FROM SECURITY TO FEAR: THE SPECTRUM EXPLORED

Safety operates on a spectrum that ranges from complete security to overwhelming fear. Each shift along this continuum profoundly affects our interactions and choices. When we feel safe, our world is one of openness and opportunity; we are more likely to take risks and embrace new experiences. In contrast, when our safety is threatened, our world contracts. We become more conservative, protective, and sometimes even paralysed by fear.

Emotions and Responses: The Hidden Depths

Our previous experiences of safety, or lack thereof, don't just fade away; they embed themselves in our emotional fabric, often resurfacing when we least expect them. For instance, if we felt unprotected or vulnerable during our formative years, these feelings could manifest later as anxiety or overcautiousness—even in completely safe situations. The emotional safety net we lacked then becomes a psychological barrier now, preventing us from stepping out of our comfort zones.

Moreover, in today's digital age, our sense of mental and emotional safety is continually challenged by social media and peer pressure. These platforms, while connecting us to the world, also expose us to judgment and scrutiny, which can evoke feelings of inadequacy or vulnerability. The shame of not measuring up can be paralysing, inhibiting us from expressing our true selves or pursuing our aspirations.

THE LINGERING IMPACT OF COMPROMISED SAFETY

Not feeling safe can create tangible obstacles in our lives. It can prevent us from pursuing new opportunities, from expressing our opinions, or from engaging fully in our relationships. When we do not feel safe, our actions are often about mitigation and defence rather than about proactive growth.

A lack of safety, while often perceived negatively, can paradoxically cultivate certain positive traits such as increased sensitivity, heightened awareness, and greater empathy. These traits can emerge as adaptive responses to environments where the perception of safety is compromised. Here’s how a lack of safety can lead to these developments:

Increased Sensitivity

When someone frequently experiences situations where their safety—physical, emotional, or psychological—is threatened, they may develop a heightened sensitivity to their surroundings. This is a survival mechanism. For example, growing up in an unstable home might make someone more attuned to subtle cues in people's moods and behaviours, enabling them to navigate their environment more cautiously. Over time, this heightened sensitivity can help them quickly identify when something or someone feels "off," which in safe environments can translate into being highly perceptive and attuned to the needs and feelings of others.

Heightened Awareness

A lack of safety often forces individuals to be more vigilant. This heightened state of alertness can evolve into a profound awareness of the dynamics and undercurrents in various situations. Such individuals are often very good at reading a room or understanding complex emotional or social interactions. This awareness is not just limited to negative cues but also extends to noticing nuances and details that others might miss, making them exceptionally mindful and observant.

Greater Empathy

Empathy often develops from experiencing or witnessing suffering and understanding vulnerability on a personal level. When someone has felt unsafe or unprotected, they know what it is like to feel exposed or at risk. This understanding can foster a deep sense of compassion for others who might be in similar situations. Empathetic individuals who have dealt with insecurity or danger are often more capable of relating to others' fears and anxieties, and they tend to be more compassionate and supportive as a result.

Practical Implications

In Personal Relationships: People who have experienced a lack of safety and have developed these traits often bring a deep sense of understanding and attentiveness to their relationships. Their ability to empathise and be sensitive to others' emotional states can make them excellent friends, partners, or caregivers.

In Professional Settings: In the workplace, such sensitivity and awareness can translate into strong interpersonal skills and the ability to manage complex social dynamics effectively. For instance, leaders who have developed empathy through personal experiences of insecurity may be better equipped to support their teams through crises.

In Social and Community Work: Heightened empathy and awareness can drive individuals to engage in social justice, community service, or counselling roles where they can use their understanding of vulnerability and their heightened perceptual skills to advocate for and help others.

While a lack of safety can undoubtedly lead to negative outcomes and challenges, it also has the potential to enhance personal growth and development in unexpected ways. By transforming these experiences into sources of strength, individuals can offer unique insights and contributions to their communities and relationships.

SAFETY AND ITS IMPACT ON ANXIETY, DEPRESSION AND NARCISSISM.

A lack of safety can have profound psychological effects, contributing to mental health challenges such as depression, anxiety, and even traits associated with narcissism. The connection between these conditions and a perceived or real absence of safety often centres around prolonged exposure to stress, unresolved trauma, and adaptive behaviours that may become maladaptive over time. Here's how these dynamics can unfold:

Depression

When an individual constantly feels unsafe, whether physically or emotionally, it can lead to chronic stress. This persistent state of heightened alertness can exhaust the body's stress response systems, leading to what is often called 'burnout' or adrenal fatigue. Over time, this chronic stress state can deplete the body's resources, leaving a person feeling drained, hopeless, and unable to derive pleasure from activities that were once enjoyable — classic symptoms of depression. Additionally, if a person's environment consistently signals danger or instability, it can foster feelings of helplessness and pessimism about the future, further embedding depressive states.

Anxiety

Anxiety is closely tied to a person's anticipatory response to threats. In environments where safety is not assured, individuals may develop an enhanced state of vigilance for potential threats. This can manifest as generalised anxiety disorder, panic disorder, or various phobias, depending on the nature of the threats experienced. The constant expectation of danger can condition the nervous system to operate as if threat is always imminent, leading to overwhelming cycles of anxiety and worry that disrupt normal functioning.

Narcissism

While narcissism is often viewed through the lens of self-aggrandisement and an inflated sense of importance, it can also be seen as a defensive adaptation to a lack of emotional safety. In this context, narcissistic behaviours may develop as a protective shell to guard against feelings of vulnerability and inadequacy.

Suppose an individual grows up in an environment where vulnerability leads to pain or betrayal. In that case, they might adopt narcissistic traits as a way to feel in control and mask their underlying insecurities. This can manifest as an excessive need for admiration, a disregard for others' feelings, and an extreme self-focus. Narcissism can be both a conscious and unconscious strategy to maintain the illusion of safety through control and dominance.

A lack of safety can significantly impact mental health by creating and perpetuating conditions that lead to depression, anxiety, and narcissism. Addressing these issues effectively requires a comprehensive understanding of the interplay between environmental factors, individual experiences, and adaptive behaviours gone awry.

PRACTICAL EXERCISES FOR ENHANCING SAFETY

Grounding Techniques: When uncertainty strikes, ground yourself by focusing on your sensory experiences. Feel the texture of what you're holding, listen to the ambient sounds, and take slow, deep breaths. Grounding helps reassure the mind that the immediate environment is secure.

Visualisation for Safety: Develop a mental safe space—an imaginary sanctuary you can visit whenever the outside world feels overwhelming. Regular visits to this mental oasis can help reinforce feelings of security and peace.

Communication Exercises: Practise expressing your needs and boundaries clearly in your relationships. Role-play scenarios where you assertively communicate your comfort levels, which can help build real-world confidence in maintaining your emotional boundaries.

RELATING SAFETY TO THE TRIANGLE OF BE-ING

Understanding safety within the framework of the Triangle of BE-ing provides a comprehensive view of how this fundamental element influences our behaviour and interactions in various contexts: when we are alone when we are affected by others, and when we influence others.

When Alone: Internal Safety

When alone, our sense of safety is deeply intertwined with our internal dialogue and self-perception. A healthy sense of safety allows for introspection and growth, enabling us to explore our thoughts and emotions without fear. This state fosters resilience and a grounded sense of self that is less prone to external fluctuations. On the other hand, if we feel unsafe even when alone, it can lead to a constant state of anxiety and distrust in one's environment and thoughts. This could manifest as paranoia, excessive worry about potential threats, or a pervasive sense of vulnerability that inhibits personal exploration and enjoyment of solitude.

WHEN AFFECTED BY OTHERS: **External Affected Safety**

Our interactions with others can significantly impact our sense of safety. When we feel safe, we're more open and able to form genuine connections, trust others, and communicate effectively. We are receptive to feedback and can handle interpersonal challenges with composure. Conversely, a lack of safety in social settings triggers defence mechanisms such as withdrawal, aggression, or compliance, which can distort genuine interactions and hinder healthy relationships. For instance, if previous relationships have compromised our sense of safety, we might enter new interactions with suspicion or nervous apprehension, which can prevent the establishment of mutual trust and respect.

WHEN INFLUENCING OTHERS: **External Affector Safety**

The environment we create around others can significantly influence their sense of safety. If we cultivate a safe environment, it can empower others to feel secure, valued, and respected, which enhances collective productivity and emotional well-being. Leaders who prioritise safety in team settings, for instance, are likely to see better engagement, creativity, and loyalty. However, if we inadvertently or intentionally create an atmosphere of being afraid to speak up, or instability, it can stifle expression, innovation, and lead to a culture of mistrust and minimal risk-taking. In family settings, parents who create a consistently safe and nurturing environment enable their children to develop secure attachment styles and healthy self-esteem.

SAFEGUARDING OUR WELL-BEING

Understanding and nurturing our need for safety allows us to navigate life's uncertainties with greater assurance and less fear. By confronting and processing our past experiences related to safety, we can break free from old fears and embrace a more empowered and secure existence. As we continue on this journey of self-discovery and growth, let's strive to create environments—both internally and externally—that foster a profound sense of safety. This foundation is not just about survival; it's about thriving.

Self-Reflection Questions on Safety.

1. What does safety mean to me personally?
2. How do I create a sense of safety in my daily life?
3. What are the key elements that make me feel safe and secure?
4. How do I respond emotionally when I feel unsafe?
5. What past experiences have shaped my perception of safety?
6. How do my relationships contribute to my sense of safety?
7. What role does my environment play in making me feel safe?
8. How do I communicate my need for safety to others?
9. What habits or routines help me maintain a sense of safety?
10. How do I handle situations where my safety is compromised?
11. In what ways do I protect my emotional safety?
12. How does my sense of safety affect my decision-making?
13. What are my boundaries, and how do they contribute to my safety?
14. How can I enhance my sense of safety without becoming overly cautious?
15. What can I do to help others feel safe around me?

CHAPTER 6 - GAIN AND LOSS

WHEN I WAS ABOUT 16 I lived at a boarding school. I had grumbling appendicitis around the time I was taking my O levels; the last year, they were offered before GCSEs came in.

While I was in hospital, I asked one of my friends to grab my wallet from the drawer in my room to keep it safe. We weren't wealthy so the little money I had was important to me.

My friend told me that someone had stolen it, and the money.

I was more upset about that than being in the hospital or missing my exams. What made it worse was that on returning to the dormitories, I found my wallet in my friend's drawer when looking for a pen to do homework. That loss of trust, confidence in him as a friend, and the connection I thought we had was worse than losing the money.

That event taught me to be wary of friends for years, and is probably one of the reasons I had so few friends growing up. I'm happy to say that is changing, especially as an avid motorbike rider in the UK, where there is a sense of community, trust and friendship wherever you go.

This experience taught me that the dynamics of gain and loss continuously shape relationships. It's not just about what we acquire or lose, but how these experiences affect our connections and emotional well-being.

THE EMOTIONAL IMPACT OF GAIN AND LOSS

Gaining something valuable, whether it's a new friend, a promotion, or achieving a personal goal, can provide a rush of positive emotions. This sense of accomplishment boosts our self-esteem and fuels our motivation. The initial euphoria can be empowering, making us feel invincible and eager to pursue further gains.

On the flip side, losing something or someone important can lead to a cascade of negative emotions. Feelings of sadness, frustration, and helplessness often accompany significant losses. Loss shakes our sense of stability and can undermine our confidence, leading to a period of emotional adjustment and recovery.

EMOTIONS WE FEEL AND RESPONSES AS A RESULT OF THIS ELEMENT

Joy and Satisfaction: When we gain, we often feel joy and satisfaction. These emotions reinforce our behaviours and motivate us to continue striving for success and connection.

Grief and Anger: Losses can evoke grief and anger. These emotions are natural responses to losing something meaningful and can lead to introspection, re-evaluation of priorities, and sometimes a drive to reclaim what was lost.

Fear and Anxiety: Both gain and loss can trigger fear of different intensities and anxiety. The concern of losing a newly acquired gain or the anxiety of never regaining something lost can dominate our thoughts and influence our actions.

Resilience and Acceptance: Over time, navigating gains and losses builds resilience. Learning to accept and adapt to these changes helps us grow emotionally and psychologically stronger.

SPECTRUM ANALYSIS: THE EMOTIONS BETWEEN GAIN AND LOSS

Between the extremes of gain and loss lies a broad spectrum of emotions that provide a nuanced understanding of our experiences. These emotions include:

Contentment and Anticipation: Contentment arises when we feel secure in our current state of gains, appreciating what we have without craving more. It's a state of satisfaction that comes from acknowledging our present situation. Anticipation, on the other hand, is the excitement and positive expectation of future gains. It drives us to set goals and strive for new achievements.

Disappointment and Regret: When our expectations are not met, disappointment sets in. It is the emotional response to not achieving what we hoped for. Regret follows when we reflect on missed opportunities or decisions that led to losses. These emotions, while often painful, are an integral part of personal growth and learning from our experiences.

Relief and Gratitude: Relief is the emotion we feel when we narrowly avoid a loss or when a difficult situation resolves favourably. It's the exhalation after holding our breath through a period of uncertainty. Gratitude is the deep appreciation for the gains we have, often heightened by the awareness of how easily these gains could be lost. Practising gratitude can transform our outlook, helping us focus on the positive aspects of our lives and enhancing our overall well-being.

HOW CAN LOSS OR GAIN LEAD TO BEING MORE SENSITIVE, AWARE, AND EMPATHETIC

Developing Sensitivity

Experiencing gain and loss significantly impacts our emotional sensitivity. When we gain something valuable, such as a new relationship or a significant achievement, we become more attuned to the nuances of joy and satisfaction. This heightened sensitivity can make us more appreciative of the positive experiences in our lives and more alert to the feelings of those around us.

Conversely, loss sharpens our sensitivity to pain and vulnerability. When we lose someone or something important, we often become more aware of similar losses in others, enhancing our ability to recognise and empathise with their suffering. This increased sensitivity can make us more compassionate and supportive friends, partners, and colleagues.

Increasing Awareness

Both gain and loss broaden our awareness of life's complexities. Gaining new experiences or resources opens our eyes to new possibilities and perspectives, enriching our understanding of the world. This broader awareness helps us navigate our personal and professional lives with greater insight and adaptability.

Loss, on the other hand, brings awareness of life's fragility and the impermanence of our circumstances. It teaches us to value what we have and to be mindful of the transient nature of success and relationships. This awareness can lead to a more grounded and balanced approach to life, where we appreciate the present moment and prepare for future uncertainties.

Enhancing Empathy

Empathy flourishes with shared experiences of gain and loss. When we celebrate our gains, we develop a deeper understanding of joy and fulfilment, which we can share with others. Celebrating together fosters a sense of community and mutual support.

Loss, however, is where empathy truly deepens. When we experience significant losses, we connect with others who have faced similar challenges. This shared vulnerability creates bonds of empathy and understanding that are difficult to forge through positive experiences alone. It's through the lens of our own pain that we can genuinely understand and support others in their struggles.

GAIN AND LOSS AND THEIR IMPACT ON ANXIETY, DEPRESSION, AND NARCISSISM

Impact on Anxiety

Anxiety often stems from the worry of potentially losing what we have gained or the uncertainty of future gains. This constant vigilance can lead to chronic stress, as individuals worry about maintaining their current status or achieving their goals. For example, someone who has recently received a promotion might feel anxious about living up to new expectations and the possibility of not meeting them, potentially leading to job insecurity.

Tips:

Mindfulness practises: Engaging in mindfulness and meditation can help manage anxiety by keeping one grounded in the present moment.

Setting Realistic Expectations: Breaking down goals into manageable steps can reduce the pressure and "fear of failure".

Impact on Depression

Significant losses, such as the end of a relationship or the death of a loved one, can trigger depressive episodes. The sense of emptiness and the perceived permanence of the loss can lead to feelings of hopelessness and despair. Depression can also follow gains if the new responsibilities or changes disrupt an individual's sense of balance or self-worth.

Tips:

Seeking help from a mental health professional, a support group or even friends can provide strategies to cope with depression.

Building Support Networks: Engaging with friends and family can offer emotional support and reduce feelings of isolation.

Go through the RAMP-IT section and decide what you can do to focus on the now, and what you can do to pursue a meaningful goal.

Impact on Narcissism

Narcissism can be fuelled by constant gains that reinforce an inflated self-image. When individuals receive continuous positive feedback, they may begin to equate their worth with their achievements, leading to an excessive focus on maintaining their status and receiving admiration. Conversely, frequent or significant losses can result in defensive narcissism, where individuals overcompensate for their perceived failures by projecting an image of superiority.

Tips:

Practising Humility: Regularly reflecting on one's actions and acknowledging the contributions of others can mitigate narcissistic tendencies.

Balanced Feedback: Seeking constructive criticism and valuing diverse perspectives helps maintain a realistic self-view.

STRATEGIES TO REMAIN BALANCED ON THE SPECTRUM

Cultivate Emotional Agility:

Flexibility in Thoughts and Feelings: Allow yourself to experience and move through emotions without being defined by them. This flexibility helps you adapt to both gains and losses effectively.

practise Appreciation:

Daily Appreciation Journaling: Regularly noting what you appreciate shifts focus from what you lack to what you have, fostering a positive mindset.

Set Realistic Expectations:

Manageable Goals: Establish achievable objectives to reduce pressure and anxiety associated with high expectations.

Develop Non-Attachment:

Appreciate Without Clinging: Enjoy gains without becoming overly attached to them, understanding that all things are temporary.

Foster Resilience:

Build Mental Strength: Engage in activities that enhance your ability to recover from setbacks, such as mindfulness, exercise, and connecting with supportive individuals.

EXERCISES TO APPRECIATE GAIN AND COPE WITH LOSS

Daily Appreciation Exercise:

Each evening, write down three things you gained that day, no matter how small. Reflecting on these gains can enhance your sense of gratitude and contentment.

Loss Processing Technique:

Allocate specific times to process feelings of loss. Reflect on the lessons learned and engage in activities that bring joy and peace afterwards, reinforcing your ability to move forward.

Visualisation for Balance:

Spend a few minutes each day visualising a scale that represents your emotional balance between gains and losses. Mentally place your experiences on this scale and find a point of equilibrium, helping you maintain emotional stability.

RELATING GAIN AND LOSS TO THE TRIANGLE OF BE-ING

Let's explore how gain and loss impact each aspect of this triangle:

When Alone (Internal): Reflecting on Personal Gains and Losses

Internal Reflection and Self-Understanding: When we are alone, we have the opportunity to reflect deeply on our personal experiences of gain and loss. This reflection helps us understand how these experiences have shaped our self-perception and worldview. For example, gaining a new skill or achieving a goal can boost our confidence and self-esteem, reinforcing our belief in our abilities. Conversely, experiencing a significant loss, such as a failed relationship or missed opportunity, can lead to introspection about our values, priorities, and resilience.

Building Resilience and Adaptability: Through this internal reflection, we can cultivate resilience and adaptability. By understanding that gains and losses are inherent parts of life, we learn to navigate them without becoming overly attached to either. This balance allows us to maintain a stable sense of self, regardless of external circumstances. Practising mindfulness and journaling can help us process emotions and gain clarity.

Personal Growth and Goal Setting: Reflecting on past gains and losses also informs our future goals and aspirations. Recognising what we've achieved helps set realistic, achievable goals, while understanding past losses guides us in avoiding previous mistakes. This continuous cycle of reflection and goal setting fosters personal growth and development.

WHEN AFFECTED **by Others (External Affected):** Observing and Reacting to Gains and Losses

Emotional Reactions to Others' Experiences: Our interactions with others significantly influence our perceptions of gain and loss. When we see friends or colleagues achieving success, it can evoke feelings of inspiration, envy, or self-reflection. Similarly, witnessing others' losses can elicit empathy, relief (for our own situation), or a deeper understanding of their struggles. These emotional reactions are a part of our social learning.

Developing Empathy and Social Awareness: Observing and reacting to others' gains and losses enhances our empathy and social awareness. Understanding the joy someone feels from a gain or the pain from a loss helps us relate to them on a deeper level. This empathy fosters stronger relationships and a supportive social network. It encourages us to be more compassionate and understanding in our interactions, promoting a more cohesive and empathetic community.

Social Comparison and Motivation: While observing others, it's natural to compare ourselves. This social comparison can be motivating or discouraging, depending on how we interpret it. Recognising that everyone experiences gains and losses helps us put our own experiences into perspective. It reminds us that success is not a linear path and that setbacks are a common part of growth. By keeping this balanced view, we can stay motivated and focused on our personal journey without being unduly influenced by others' achievements or failures.

WHEN INFLUENCING OTHERS (EXTERNAL AFFECTOR): Impacting Others' Perceptions of Gain and Loss

Modelling Resilience and Positivity: How we handle our own gains and losses can serve as a powerful model for those around us. By demonstrating resilience in the face of loss and humility in times of gain, we set a positive example. This behaviour encourages others to adopt similar attitudes, creating a ripple effect of resilience and balanced emotional responses within our community. Sharing stories of overcoming adversity and celebrating achievements without arrogance can inspire and uplift others.

Creating Supportive Environments: As influencers in our social circles, we have the ability to create environments that are supportive and nurturing. Acknowledging and celebrating others' gains fosters a sense of community and shared joy. Offering support and understanding during times of loss helps others feel valued and understood. This supportive environment enhances collective well-being and fosters a culture of mutual respect and empathy.

Encouraging Balanced Perspectives:

Our influence can help others develop balanced perspectives on gain and loss. By encouraging open discussions about both successes and failures, we help demystify the emotional rollercoaster associated with these experiences. This transparency promotes a healthy approach to handling life's ups and downs. Encouraging reflective practises, such as gratitude or appreciation journaling and loss processing, can further aid others in maintaining emotional equilibrium.

INTEGRATING THE TRIANGLE OF BE-ING INTO DAILY LIFE

To effectively integrate the Triangle of BE-ing with the concepts of gain and loss, consider the following practical steps:

Internal Reflection:

Daily Journaling: Reflect on daily gains and losses, noting the emotions they evoke and the lessons learned.

Mindfulness Meditation: practise mindfulness to stay present and balanced, especially during significant gains or losses.

Social Interactions:

Active Listening: Be fully present when others share their experiences of gain and loss, offering empathy and support.

Celebrate Others: Acknowledge and celebrate others' successes, fostering a positive and supportive community.

Influencing Others:

Share Your Stories: Openly share your own experiences of gain and loss, highlighting both the struggles and the growth.

Encourage Resilience: Promote resilience by discussing how you overcome setbacks and maintain balance.

Understanding how gain and loss influence and are influenced by the Triangle of BE-ing offers a comprehensive framework for navigating life's emotional landscape. By reflecting internally, engaging empathetically with others, and positively influencing our social circles, we can cultivate a balanced, resilient approach to life's inevitable fluctuations. This holistic perspective not only enhances our personal growth but also fosters stronger, more supportive communities.

SELF-REFLECTION QUESTIONS FOR THE STATE/SENSE OF GAIN AND LOSS

1. How do I typically react to gains and achievements in my life?
2. What emotions do I experience when I lose something important?
3. How do I balance my response to gains and losses?
4. What have been the most significant gains in my life, and how have they impacted me?
5. How have significant losses shaped my perspective on life?
6. How do I process and cope with feelings of grief and loss?
7. In what ways do gains motivate me to pursue my goals?
8. How do losses influence my sense of resilience and adaptability?
9. What lessons have I learned from past gains and losses?
10. How do I celebrate my gains without becoming overconfident?
11. How can I develop a healthier relationship with both gain and loss?
12. How do I support others in their experiences of gain and loss?

13. What role does gratitude play in how I perceive gains and losses?
14. How do my expectations affect my emotional response to gain and loss?
15. How can I use my experiences of gain and loss to foster personal growth?

CHAPTER 7 - CLARITY AND CONFUSION

UNPACKING CLARITY AND CONFUSION: A PERSONAL STORY

WHEN I WAS in my early twenties, I faced a pivotal career decision that would shape my professional future. I had two job offers: one from a well-established company with a clear career path and another from a startup with an uncertain future but a lot of potential for innovation and growth. The established company promised stability, a structured environment, and a clear trajectory for advancement. The startup, however, offered a dynamic work culture, the excitement of building something new, and the potential for significant professional growth.

This decision weighed heavily on me. I spent countless sleepless nights and created numerous pros and cons lists, trying to see which option aligned more with my personal and professional values. The confusion I felt was overwhelming, as each option seemed to offer unique benefits and challenges. I decided to take a step back and reflect deeply on my long-term aspirations, values, and what I wanted to achieve in life.

Through this process, I began to find clarity. I realised that my passion for innovation and growth aligned more with the startup's environment. I chose the startup, and this decision brought a profound sense of empowerment and confidence. The clarity I achieved not only helped me make the decision but also strengthened my resolve and commitment to my chosen path.

This experience taught me the powerful impact that clarity and confusion have on our lives. It's not just about making decisions but understanding how these states influence our emotional well-being and relationships.

THE EMOTIONAL IMPACT OF CLARITY AND CONFUSION

Positive Emotions from Clarity

When we achieve clarity, it brings a wave of positive emotions. Clarity instills a sense of confidence and assurance, making us feel more capable and self-reliant. This newfound confidence often leads to a boost in self-esteem, as we become more certain of our decisions and actions. With clarity, our minds are free from the clutter of uncertainty, allowing us to focus more effectively on our goals. This focused mindset enhances our motivation and productivity, as we are no longer distracted by doubts or indecision. The sense of direction that clarity provides can be empowering, making us feel more in control of our lives and our futures.

Negative Emotions from Confusion

Conversely, confusion can be a source of significant emotional distress. When we are confused, it often leads to feelings of anxiety and doubt. The uncertainty about the right course of action can be paralyzing, making it difficult to make decisions or move forward. This state of confusion can undermine our confidence, leading to a sense of helplessness and frustration. Persistent confusion can also create a mental fog, where our thoughts feel scattered and our ability to concentrate is diminished. This mental state can be draining, both emotionally and physically, as we expend energy trying to navigate the murky waters of uncertainty.

EMOTIONS WE FEEL AND RESPONSES AS A RESULT OF THIS ELEMENT

Confidence and Assurance

When we experience clarity, it brings confidence and assurance. These positive emotions reinforce our actions and decisions, creating a virtuous cycle of growth and achievement. With clarity, we feel more certain of our path and our choices, which boosts our self-esteem and encourages us to take decisive action. This confidence helps us tackle challenges head-on, as we believe in our ability to succeed. The assurance that comes with clarity also fosters a sense of peace and stability, as we are no longer plagued by doubts or fears.

Anxiety and Doubt

On the other hand, confusion often brings anxiety and doubt. These negative emotions can create a vicious cycle of indecision and inaction. When we are unsure of our path, we start to question our abilities and our choices, which leads to further confusion and hesitation. This state of doubt can be crippling, making it difficult to take any action for fear of making the wrong choice. The anxiety that accompanies confusion can also manifest physically, with symptoms such as increased heart rate, sweating, and a sense of dread. This constant state of worry can be exhausting, draining our energy and focus.

Relief and Satisfaction

Achieving clarity after a period of confusion brings immense relief and satisfaction. The transition from uncertainty to understanding is incredibly rewarding, as it validates our efforts and perseverance. This relief is often accompanied by a sense of accomplishment, as we have successfully navigated through confusion to reach a clear decision. The satisfaction that follows is profound, as we can now move forward with confidence and purpose. This emotional shift from confusion to clarity can also renew our motivation and drive, as we feel more capable and empowered.

Frustration and Overwhelm

Persistent confusion can lead to frustration and overwhelm. These emotions can drain our energy and motivation, making it difficult to move forward and achieve our goals. When we are confused, every decision can feel like an insurmountable challenge, leading to a sense of frustration and helplessness. This frustration can spill over into other areas of our lives, affecting our relationships and our overall well-being. The feeling of being overwhelmed by confusion can also create a mental block, where we struggle to think clearly or make any progress. This state of overwhelm can be paralyzing, trapping us in a cycle of inaction and frustration.

SPECTRUM ANALYSIS: THE EMOTIONS BETWEEN CLARITY AND CONFUSION

Certainty and Confidence

Certainty brings confidence. When we are clear about our goals and the steps needed to achieve them, we feel empowered and self-assured. This sense of certainty provides a solid foundation for our actions, allowing us to move forward with determination and purpose. Confidence follows naturally, as we believe in our ability to succeed and achieve our goals. This positive feedback loop of certainty and confidence can drive us to new heights, as we pursue our aspirations with clarity and focus.

Ambiguity and Hesitation

Ambiguity often leads to hesitation. When we are unsure about our path, it becomes difficult to take decisive action, and we may find ourselves stuck in a state of indecision. This ambiguity can create a sense of unease, as we grapple with the unknown and the uncertain. Hesitation follows, as we struggle to make decisions or commit to a course of action. This state of limbo can be frustrating and demoralising, as we feel trapped by our inability to move forward.

Assurance and Determination

Assurance comes from clarity, fostering determination. When we are certain of our direction, we can pursue our goals with unwavering resolve. This assurance provides a sense of stability and confidence, which fuels our determination to succeed. With clarity, we can set clear, achievable goals and develop a focused plan of action. This determination helps us overcome obstacles and stay committed to our path, as we are driven by a clear sense of purpose and direction.

Uncertainty and Indecisiveness

Uncertainty breeds indecisiveness. The lack of clarity makes it challenging to commit to a course of action, leading to procrastination and self-doubt. This state of uncertainty can create a sense of paralysis, where every decision feels fraught with risk and potential failure. Indecisiveness follows, as we struggle to make choices or take action. This can lead to missed opportunities and a sense of stagnation, as we are unable to move forward with confidence and purpose.

HOW CAN CLARITY OR CONFUSION LEAD TO BEING MORE SENSITIVE, AWARE, AND EMPATHETIC

Developing Mental Clarity

Experiencing clarity enhances our sensitivity to positive experiences and emotions. When we achieve clarity, we become more attuned to the feelings of confidence and assurance. This heightened sensitivity helps us appreciate our achievements and recognise the clarity in others' actions and decisions. Clarity allows us to see things more clearly, understand our own motivations and values, and appreciate the positive aspects of our lives. This increased sensitivity can make us more empathetic and understanding, as we are better able to recognise and appreciate the clarity and confidence in others.

Increasing Awareness Through Reflection

Both clarity and confusion broaden our awareness. Clarity helps us see things more clearly and understand the nuances of our goals and aspirations. When we are clear about our path, we can reflect more deeply on our motivations, values, and the steps needed to achieve our goals. Confusion, on the other hand, forces us to reflect and dig deeper into our thoughts and feelings, increasing our self-awareness. This reflection helps us understand the root causes of our confusion, identify patterns in our thinking, and develop strategies to achieve clarity. This increased awareness can lead to greater personal growth and a deeper understanding of ourselves and our aspirations.

Enhancing Empathy Through Understanding

Understanding our own experiences of clarity and confusion helps us empathise with others. When we see someone struggling with confusion, we can relate to their feelings and offer support and guidance. We recognise the pain and frustration that comes with confusion and can provide a listening ear or helpful advice. Similarly, witnessing others' clarity can inspire and motivate us to seek our own clarity. Seeing someone else achieve clarity can give us hope and encouragement, as we realise that clarity is attainable and worth striving for. This shared understanding of clarity and confusion fosters empathy and connection, as we relate to others' experiences on a deeper level.

CLARITY AND CONFUSION AND THEIR IMPACT ON ANXIETY, DEPRESSION, AND NARCISSISM

Impact on Anxiety

Anxiety often stems from confusion and uncertainty. The worry about making the wrong decision or not finding clarity can lead to chronic stress. This constant state of vigilance can be exhausting, as we are always on edge, fearing the unknown. Anxiety can also create a cycle of worry and inaction, where the fear of making a mistake prevents us from taking any action at all.

Tips for Managing Anxiety:

- **Mindfulness practises:** Engaging in mindfulness and meditation can help manage anxiety by keeping us grounded in the present moment. These practises teach us to observe our thoughts without judgment and to focus on the here and now, reducing the power of anxiety.
- **Setting Realistic Expectations:** Breaking down goals into manageable steps can reduce the pressure and "fear of failure." By setting achievable objectives, we can build confidence and momentum, reducing the anxiety associated with high expectations.

Impact on Depression

Significant confusion, especially if prolonged, can trigger depressive episodes. The sense of being lost or unable to find clarity can lead to feelings of hopelessness and despair. Depression can also follow from a perceived failure to achieve clarity or from the overwhelming burden of persistent confusion. This state of mind can drain our energy and motivation, making it difficult to see a way forward.

Tips for Coping with Depression:

Seeking Professional Help: Talking to a mental health professional can provide strategies to cope with depression. Therapists can offer techniques and support to navigate through depressive feelings and find ways to achieve clarity.

Building Support Networks: Engaging with friends and family can offer emotional support and reduce feelings of isolation. Sharing our experiences with trusted individuals can provide comfort and new perspectives, helping us feel less alone in our struggles.

Use the RAMPIT Self Coaching framework: A benefit of knowing how to self-coach, which you'll learn later in the book, is the ability to define a goal or purpose and reflect on what your doing in relation to that. Depression often rears it's head when you don't have a purpose or goal to lean in to.

IMPACT ON NARCISSISM

Narcissism can be fueled by clarity that reinforces an inflated self-image. When individuals receive continuous validation, they may begin to equate their worth with their clarity and achievements. This can lead to an excessive focus on maintaining their status and receiving admiration. Conversely, frequent or significant confusion can result in defensive narcissism, where individuals overcompensate for their perceived failures by projecting an image of superiority.

TIPS FOR MITIGATING NARCISSISTIC TENDENCIES:

- **Practising Humility:** Regularly reflecting on one's actions and acknowledging the contributions of others can mitigate narcissistic tendencies. This practise helps maintain a balanced and realistic self-view, recognising that achievements are often the result of collective effort.
- **Balanced Feedback:** Seeking constructive criticism and valuing diverse perspectives helps maintain a realistic self-view. By embracing feedback and learning from it, individuals can develop a more grounded and humble approach to their achievements.

STRATEGIES TO REMAIN BALANCED ON THE SPECTRUM

Cultivate Emotional Agility

Flexibility in Thoughts and Feelings: Allow yourself to experience and move through emotions without being defined by them. This flexibility helps you adapt to both clarity and confusion effectively. By recognising that emotions are transient, you can navigate through them with greater ease and resilience.

practise Gratitude and Appreciation

Daily Appreciation Journaling: Regularly noting what you appreciate shifts focus from what you lack to what you have, fostering a positive mindset. This practise helps cultivate a sense of contentment and appreciation, enhancing overall well-being.

Set Realistic Expectations

Manageable Goals: Establish achievable objectives to reduce pressure and anxiety associated with high expectations. Setting realistic goals helps build confidence and a sense of accomplishment, which can mitigate the negative effects of confusion.

Develop Cognitive Flexibility

Adaptable Thinking: Cultivate the ability to change your thinking patterns and perspectives, which helps in navigating both clarity and confusion. Cognitive flexibility allows you to approach problems from different angles and find creative solutions.

Foster Resilience

Build Mental Strength: Engage in activities that enhance your ability to recover from setbacks, such as mindfulness, exercise, and connecting with supportive individuals. Resilience helps you bounce back from confusion and maintain a positive outlook.

EXERCISES TO CULTIVATE CLARITY AND MANAGE CONFUSION

Daily Clarity practise

Each evening, write down three things you achieved that day and the clarity they brought you. Reflecting on these achievements can enhance your sense of purpose and direction. This practise helps reinforce positive experiences and build confidence.

Confusion Processing Technique

Allocate specific times to process feelings of confusion. Reflect on the causes and potential solutions, and engage in activities that bring joy and peace afterward, reinforcing your ability to move forward. This structured approach helps you manage confusion and find clarity.

Visualisation for Mental Clarity

Spend a few minutes each day visualising a clear path or a light breaking through fog, representing your mental clarity. This mental exercise helps reinforce your ability to achieve clarity and maintain focus.

RELATING CLARITY AND CONFUSION TO THE TRIANGLE OF BE-ING

When Alone (Internal)

Internal Reflection and Self-Understanding: When we are alone, we have the opportunity to reflect deeply on our personal experiences of clarity and confusion. This reflection helps us understand how these experiences have shaped our self-perception and worldview. By exploring our thoughts and emotions, we gain insight into our motivations, values, and goals.

Building Mental Clarity and Adaptability: Through this internal reflection, we can cultivate mental clarity and adaptability. By understanding that clarity and confusion are inherent parts of life, we learn to navigate them without becoming overly attached to either. Practicing mindfulness and journaling in this process, help us process emotions and gain clarity.

Personal Growth and Decision-Making: Reflecting on past clarity and confusion also informs our future goals and aspirations. Recognising what we've achieved helps set realistic, achievable goals, while understanding past confusion guides us in avoiding previous mistakes. This continuous cycle of reflection and goal setting fosters personal growth and development.

WHEN AFFECTED **by Others (External Affected)**

Emotional Reactions to Others' Clarity and Confusion: Our interactions with others significantly influence our perceptions of clarity and confusion. When we see friends or colleagues achieving clarity, it can evoke feelings of inspiration, envy, or self-reflection. Similarly, witnessing others' confusion can elicit empathy, relief (for our own situation), or a deeper understanding of their struggles.

Developing Empathy and Social Awareness: Observing and reacting to others' clarity and confusion enhances our empathy and social awareness. Understanding the joy someone feels from clarity or the pain from confusion helps us relate to them on a deeper level. This empathy fosters stronger relationships and a supportive social network. It encourages us to be more compassionate and understanding in our interactions, promoting a more cohesive and empathetic community.

Social Comparison and Motivation: While observing others, it's natural to compare ourselves. This social comparison can be motivating or discouraging, depending on how we interpret it. Recognising that everyone experiences clarity and confusion helps us put our own experiences into perspective. It reminds us that success is not a linear path and that setbacks are a common part of growth. By keeping this balanced view, we can stay motivated and focused on our personal journey without being unduly influenced by others' achievements or failures.

WHEN INFLUENCING **Others (External Affector)**

Modelling Clarity and Positivity: How we handle our own clarity and confusion can serve as a powerful model for those around us. By demonstrating resilience in the face of confusion and humility in times of clarity, we set a positive example. This behaviour encourages others to adopt similar attitudes, creating a ripple effect of resilience and balanced emotional responses within our community. Sharing stories of overcoming confusion and celebrating clarity without arrogance can inspire and uplift others.

Creating Supportive Environments: As influencers in our social circles, we have the ability to create environments that are supportive and nurturing. Acknowledging and celebrating others' clarity fosters a sense of community and shared joy. Offering support and understanding during times of confusion helps others feel valued and understood. This supportive environment enhances collective well-being and fosters a culture of mutual respect and empathy.

Encouraging Balanced Perspectives: Our influence can help others develop balanced perspectives on clarity and confusion. By encouraging open discussions about both successes and failures, we help demystify the emotional rollercoaster associated with these experiences. This transparency promotes a healthy approach to handling life's ups and downs. Encouraging reflective practises, such as gratitude journaling and confusion processing, can further aid others in maintaining emotional equilibrium.

INTEGRATING THE TRIANGLE OF BE-ING INTO DAILY LIFE

Internal Reflection

- **Daily Journaling:** Reflect on daily clarity and confusion, noting the emotions they evoke, and the lessons learned. This practise helps cultivate self-awareness and personal growth.
- **Mindfulness Meditation:** practise mindfulness to stay present and balanced, especially during significant clarity or confusion. Mindfulness helps manage stress and enhance emotional regulation.

Social Interactions

- **Active Listening:** Be fully present when others share their experiences of clarity and confusion, offering empathy and support. This practise fosters deeper connections and understanding.

- **Celebrate Others:** Acknowledge and celebrate others' achievements and moments of clarity, fostering a positive and supportive community. Sharing in others' joy enhances mutual respect and camaraderie.

Influencing Others

- **Share Your Stories:** Openly share your own experiences of clarity and confusion, highlighting both the struggles and the growth. This transparency encourages others to embrace their own journeys and learn from them.
- **Encourage Resilience and Clarity:** Promote resilience by discussing how you overcome setbacks and maintain clarity. Encourage others to develop their own strategies for achieving and maintaining clarity.

Understanding how clarity and confusion influence and are influenced by the Triangle of BE-ing offers a comprehensive framework for navigating life's emotional landscape. By reflecting internally, engaging empathetically with others, and positively influencing our social circles, we can cultivate a balanced, resilient approach to life's inevitable fluctuations. This holistic perspective not only enhances our personal growth but also fosters stronger, more supportive communities.

SELF-REFLECTION QUESTIONS ON THE STATE/SENSE OF CLARITY AND CONFUSION.

1. What does clarity mean to me, and how do I achieve it?
2. How do I typically respond to feelings of confusion?
3. What practises help me find clarity in confusing situations?
4. How does clarity affect my emotional well-being and decision-making?

5. How do I distinguish between moments of clarity and confusion in my life?
6. What role does self-reflection play in achieving clarity?
7. How do I handle the anxiety that comes with confusion?
8. In what areas of my life do I feel the most clarity?
9. How do I maintain clarity when faced with conflicting information or opinions?
10. What strategies do I use to overcome periods of confusion?
11. How does my sense of clarity impact my relationships with others?
12. How do I balance the need for clarity with the acceptance of uncertainty?
13. How can I use confusion as a learning opportunity?
14. What external factors influence my sense of clarity and confusion?
15. How can I support others who are experiencing confusion?

CHAPTER 8 - SELF AND EGO

I CRIED as I started writing this book and I'm not ashamed to admit it. On some level, it felt a bit overwhelming, having this idea or philosophy and believing that people might actually want to read it and get something from it. I wrote the introduction and part of the first chapter and sent it to a few people I trusted. People I know who would tear it apart if it didn't make sense, in a loving but honest way of course. They loved it. That's what made me cry. One of them called me, crying, as she was going through something that morning and just reading the beginning of this helped her see why she had reacted in an unhelpful way for both her and the other person.

My initial thoughts were "Am I good enough to write this?", "What will the experts think?" "What will the trolls say?"

And then I remembered what I was writing a book about, had a quick chat with myself, made a fresh cup of tea and wrote the rest of the outline, still sitting on the settee in my dressing gown having not moved since the idea popped in my head that morning, except to make my cuppa and let the dog out!

I didn't share this story for you to feel any kind of emotions for me. It was to show that even when you know this stuff, thoughts still happen. Emotions still happen. It's knowing how to recognise the emotions that may be limiting you and being able to say, "Whoa, hold on a minute, Bessie, you're not going anywhere with that!" and reigning it in so you can continue your path unhindered.

THE EMOTIONAL IMPACT OF SELF AND EGO

Positive Emotions from a Healthy Sense of Self

A healthy sense of self fosters positive emotions such as self-respect, authenticity, and contentment. When we are in tune with our true selves, we experience a deep sense of fulfilment and inner peace. This authenticity allows us to engage in meaningful relationships and pursue our goals with integrity. We feel confident and self-assured, knowing that our actions align with our values and beliefs. This inner harmony enhances our overall well-being and promotes a positive outlook on life.

Negative Emotions from an Inflated Ego

An inflated ego, on the other hand, can lead to negative emotions such as arrogance, insecurity, and envy. When our ego becomes dominant, we may prioritise our self-image over genuine connections and achievements. This can create a constant need for validation and recognition, leading to feelings of inadequacy and defensiveness when these needs are not met. The pursuit of ego-driven goals can also lead to stress and burnout, as we strive to maintain an unrealistic standard of perfection.

EMOTIONS WE FEEL AND RESPONSES AS A RESULT OF THIS ELEMENT

Self-Respect and Authenticity

A balanced sense of self fosters self-respect and authenticity. These emotions encourage us to honour our true selves and engage in honest, meaningful interactions. Self-respect comes from recognising our inherent worth and setting boundaries that protect our well-being. Authenticity involves being true to ourselves and expressing our thoughts and feelings openly. These qualities promote healthy relationships and personal fulfillment.

Pride and Arrogance

While a healthy sense of self can lead to pride in our achievements, an inflated ego can turn this pride into arrogance. Arrogance involves an exaggerated sense of self-importance and superiority over others. This emotion can alienate us from others and create conflicts in our relationships. It's important to balance pride with humility, recognising that our achievements are often the result of collective effort and support.

Humility and Gratitude

Humility and gratitude are essential for maintaining a balanced sense of self. Humility involves acknowledging our limitations and valuing the contributions of others. Gratitude helps us appreciate the support and opportunities we receive, fostering a positive and generous mindset. These emotions counteract the negative effects of ego and promote a more grounded and compassionate outlook on life.

Insecurity and Envy

Insecurity and envy often stem from an inflated ego. When we compare ourselves to others and feel threatened by their success, we can feel inadequacy and resentment. These emotions can damage our self-esteem and strain our relationships. Developing self-awareness and practising self-compassion can help mitigate these negative feelings and promote a healthier sense of self.

SPECTRUM ANALYSIS: THE EMOTIONS BETWEEN HEALTHY SELF AND INFLATED EGO

Self-Assurance and Overconfidence

Self-assurance comes from a healthy sense of self, providing a stable foundation for our actions and decisions. Overconfidence, however, results from an inflated ego and can lead to reckless or arrogant behaviour. Balancing self-assurance with humility ensures that we remain confident without becoming overbearing.

Self-Worth and Entitlement

A healthy sense of self fosters a strong sense of self-worth, recognising our inherent value. Entitlement, on the other hand, stems from an inflated ego and involves an excessive sense of deservingness. This can lead to unrealistic expectations and dissatisfaction when our demands are not met. Practising humility helps maintain a balanced perspective.

Self-Acceptance and Vanity

Self-acceptance involves embracing our strengths and weaknesses and fostering a sense of inner peace. Vanity, driven by ego, focuses on outward appearances and external validation. This can create a superficial and unstable sense of self-worth. Developing self-compassion and focusing on inner qualities promotes genuine self-acceptance.

Contentment and Overvaluation

Contentment arises from a balanced sense of self, appreciating our achievements without overvaluing them. Overvaluation, driven by ego, involves an exaggerated sense of importance and entitlement. When our expectations are not met, this can lead to disappointment and dissatisfaction.

Disappointment and Defensiveness

Disappointment and defensiveness often occur when our ego-driven expectations are not met. These emotions can create conflicts and strain relationships. Developing self-awareness and practising self-compassion can help us manage these feelings and respond more constructively.

Relief and Self-Criticism

Relief follows the release of ego-driven pressures and expectations. Self-criticism, however, can undermine our sense of self-worth. Balancing self-reflection with self-compassion helps us learn from our experiences without becoming overly critical.

Self-Awareness and Narcissism

Self-awareness is the foundation of a healthy sense of self, enabling us to understand our emotions, motivations, and behaviours. Narcissism, resulting from an inflated ego, involves an excessive preoccupation with oneself and a lack of empathy for others. Practising mindfulness and seeking feedback from others can enhance self-awareness and mitigate narcissistic tendencies.

HOW CAN UNDERSTANDING SELF AND EGO LEAD TO BEING MORE SENSITIVE, AWARE, AND EMPATHETIC

Developing Authenticity

Understanding and balancing self and ego enhances our authenticity. When we embrace our true selves, we become more attuned to our values, emotions, and motivations. This authenticity allows us to engage in genuine interactions and build deeper connections with others. It also fosters a sense of inner peace and fulfillment, as we are no longer driven by ego-driven desires.

Increasing Self-Awareness

A healthy balance between self and ego increases self-awareness. By reflecting on our thoughts and behaviours, we can identify areas where our ego may be influencing our actions. This awareness helps us make conscious choices that align with our true selves. It also allows us to recognise and address negative emotions, such as insecurity and envy, promoting emotional regulation and well-being.

Enhancing Empathy Through Humility

Balancing self and ego enhances our empathy for others. When we practise humility, we become more aware of others' experiences and perspectives. This empathy fosters stronger relationships and a supportive community. By valuing others and recognising their contributions, we create an environment of mutual respect and understanding. This enhances our ability to connect with others on a deeper level and provide meaningful support.

SELF AND EGO AND THEIR IMPACT ON ANXIETY, DEPRESSION, AND RELATIONSHIPS

Impact on Anxiety

Ego-driven anxiety often stems from the fear of not meeting our own or others' expectations. This constant need for validation can create chronic stress and undermine our well-being.

Tips for Managing Ego-Related Anxiety:

Mindfulness practises: Engaging in mindfulness and meditation can help manage anxiety by keeping us grounded in the present moment. These practises teach us to observe our thoughts without judgment and reduce the power of ego-driven fears.

Setting Realistic Expectations: Setting achievable goals and focusing on our intrinsic values can reduce the pressure and anxiety associated with ego-driven expectations.

Impact on Depression

Issues with self-worth, often exacerbated by an inflated ego, can trigger depressive episodes. When our sense of self is tied to external validation, failures or criticisms can lead to feelings of hopelessness and despair.

Tips for Coping with Self-Worth Issues:

Seeking Professional Help: Talking to a mental health professional can provide strategies to cope with depression and issues related to self-worth. Therapists can help us develop a healthier sense of self and manage ego-driven emotions.

Building Support Networks: Engaging with friends and family can offer emotional support and reduce feelings of isolation. Sharing our experiences with trusted individuals can provide comfort and new perspectives, helping us feel less alone in our struggles.

Impact on Relationships

An inflated ego can strain relationships by creating conflicts and reducing empathy. Balancing self and ego promotes healthier, more supportive relationships.

Tips for Maintaining Healthy Relationships:

Practicing Humility: Regularly reflecting on one's actions and acknowledging the contributions of others can foster humility and improve relationships. This practise helps us value others and create a supportive environment.

Active Listening: Being fully present and attentive when others share their experiences fosters deeper connections and mutual respect. This practise enhances our empathy and understanding, promoting healthier relationships.

STRATEGIES TO MAINTAIN A BALANCED SENSE OF SELF

Cultivate Self-Awareness

Regular self-reflection helps us understand our emotions, motivations, and behaviours. This awareness allows us to identify when our ego may be influencing our actions and make conscious choices that align with our true selves.

practise Self-Compassion

Being kind to ourselves, especially during times of failure or criticism, helps maintain a balanced sense of self. Self-compassion fosters emotional resilience and reduces the negative impact of ego-driven emotions.

Set Realistic Self-Expectations

Establishing achievable goals and focusing on intrinsic values helps reduce the pressure and anxiety associated with high expectations. This practise promotes a healthier, more balanced sense of self.

Develop Humility and Gratitude

Practising humility and gratitude helps counteract the negative effects of an inflated ego. These qualities foster a positive and generous mind-set, enhancing our overall well-being.

Foster Resilience

Engaging in activities that enhance our ability to recover from setbacks, such as mindfulness, exercise, and connecting with supportive individuals, builds resilience. This resilience helps us navigate the challenges of balancing self and ego effectively.

EXERCISES TO STRENGTHEN A HEALTHY SELF AND MANAGE EGO

Daily Self-Reflection practise

Each evening, reflect on your actions and motivations, noting moments when your ego may have influenced your behaviour. This practise enhances self-awareness and promotes a balanced sense of self.

Ego-Check Technique

When faced with a decision or conflict, ask yourself if your actions are driven by your true self or by ego. This technique helps you make more authentic and conscious choices.

Visualisation for a Balanced Self

Spend a few minutes each day visualising a balance between your true self and your ego. This mental exercise helps reinforce your ability to maintain a healthy sense of self.

RELATING SELF AND EGO TO THE TRIANGLE OF BE-ING

When Alone (Internal)

Internal Reflection and Self-Understanding: When we are alone, we have the opportunity to reflect deeply on our personal experiences of self and ego. This reflection helps us understand how these experiences have shaped our self-perception and worldview. By exploring our thoughts and emotions, we gain insight into our motivations, values, and goals.

Building Authenticity and Self-Acceptance: Through this internal reflection, we can cultivate authenticity and self-acceptance. By understanding that self and ego are inherent parts of life, we learn to navigate them without becoming overly attached to either.

Personal Growth and Ego Management: Reflecting on past experiences of self and ego also informs our future goals and aspirations. Recognising what we've achieved helps set realistic, achievable goals, while understanding past ego-driven behaviours guides us in avoiding previous mistakes. This continuous cycle of reflection and goal **setting fosters personal growth and development.**

WHEN AFFECTED **by Others (External Affected)**

Emotional Reactions to Others' Ego and Self-Perception:

Our interactions with others significantly influence our perceptions of self and ego. When we see friends or colleagues exhibiting ego-driven behaviour, it can evoke feelings of frustration, envy, or self-reflection. Similarly, witnessing others' authenticity can inspire and motivate us to seek our own authenticity.

Developing Empathy and Social Awareness: Observing and reacting to others' self and ego enhances our empathy and social awareness. Understanding the impact of ego on others' behaviour helps us relate to them on a deeper level. This empathy fosters stronger relationships and a supportive social network. It encourages us to be more compassionate and understanding in our interactions, promoting a more cohesive and empathetic community.

Social Comparison and Motivation: While observing others, it's natural to compare ourselves. This social comparison can be motivating or discouraging, depending on how we interpret it. Recognising that everyone experiences ego-driven behaviour helps us put our own experiences into perspective. It reminds us that success is not a linear path and that setbacks are a common part of growth. By keeping this balanced view, we can stay motivated and focused on our personal journey without being unduly influenced by others' achievements or failures.

WHEN INFLUENCING **Others (External Affector)**

Modeling Humility and Authenticity: How we handle our own self and ego can serve as a powerful model for those around us. By demonstrating humility in the face of success and authenticity in our interactions, we set a positive example. This behaviour encourages others to adopt similar attitudes, creating a ripple effect of authenticity and balanced emotional responses within our community. Sharing stories of overcoming ego-driven challenges and celebrating authenticity without arrogance can inspire and uplift others.

Creating Supportive Environments: As influencers in our social circles, we have the ability to create environments that are supportive and nurturing. Acknowledging and celebrating others' authenticity fosters a sense of community and shared joy. Offering support and understanding during times of ego-driven challenges helps others feel valued and understood. This supportive environment enhances collective well-being and fosters a culture of mutual respect and empathy.

Encouraging Balanced Perspectives: Our influence can help others develop balanced perspectives on self and ego. By encouraging open discussions about both successes and failures, we help demystify the emotional rollercoaster associated with these experiences. This transparency promotes a healthy approach to handling life's ups and downs. Encouraging reflective practises, such as ego-checking, can further aid others in maintaining emotional equilibrium.

INTEGRATING THE TRIANGLE OF BE-ING INTO DAILY LIFE

Internal Reflection

Daily Journaling: Reflect on daily experiences of self and ego, noting the emotions they evoke, and the lessons learned. This practise helps cultivate self-awareness and personal growth.

Mindfulness Meditation: practise mindfulness to stay present and balanced, especially during significant ego-driven challenges. Mindfulness helps manage stress and enhance emotional regulation.

Social Interactions

Active Listening: Be fully present when others share their experiences of self and ego, offering empathy and support. This practise fosters deeper connections and mutual respect.

Celebrating Authenticity: Acknowledge and celebrate others' authenticity, fostering a positive and supportive community. Sharing in others' genuine experiences enhances mutual respect and camaraderie.

Influencing Others

Share Your Stories: Openly share your own experiences of self and ego, highlighting both the struggles and the growth. This transparency encourages others to embrace their own journeys and learn from them.

Encourage Authenticity and Humility: Promote authenticity and humility by discussing how you manage ego-driven challenges and maintain a balanced sense of self. Encourage others to develop their own strategies for achieving and maintaining authenticity.

Understanding how self and ego influence and are influenced by the Triangle of BE-ing offers a comprehensive framework for navigating life's emotional landscape. By reflecting internally, engaging empathetically with others, and positively influencing our social circles, we can cultivate a balanced, resilient approach to life's inevitable fluctuations. This holistic perspective not only enhances our personal growth but also fosters stronger, more supportive communities.

Self-Reflection Questions For The State/Sense Of Self vs Ego

1. How do I define my sense of self, and what contributes to it?
2. What role does my ego play in my daily interactions and decisions?
3. How do I differentiate between my true self and my ego-driven desires?
4. In what ways does my ego help or hinder my personal growth?
5. How do I handle situations where my ego is challenged or threatened?
6. How do I practise humility and gratitude in my daily life?
7. What experiences have shaped my understanding of self and ego?
8. How do I maintain a balanced sense of self without becoming egocentric?
9. What strategies do I use to keep my ego in check?
10. How does my ego influence my relationships with others?
11. In what ways can I cultivate a healthier sense of self?
12. How do I respond to criticism or failure, and what does that say about my ego?
13. How can I develop greater self-awareness and authenticity?

14. What practises help me stay grounded and connected to my true self?
15. How can I support others in their journey of self-discovery and ego management?

PART THREE

CHAPTER 9 - THE EXPERIENCE LOOP

UNDERSTANDING THE EXPERIENCE LOOP

Take a deep breath in. And out. Remember to stop, check in with yourself, your body, your thoughts, your emotions, and … breathe. Drink some water too, it'll help!

The Experience Loop is an important framework that illustrates the continuous cycle of perception, response, and adaptation in our behaviour and emotional dynamics. By examining each stage of this loop, we can gain insight into our behaviours, recognise patterns, and make intentional changes that enhance our emotional well-being and overall satisfaction with life.

THE EXPERIENCE LOOP CONSISTS OF FIVE STAGES:

1. **Existing State**: This is your current emotional, mental, and physical state developed from everything you've learned and processed from birth until today. It's essentially the "this is

who I am" statement, or rather, "who I've learned to be." Your existing state is shaped by your past experiences and how you have processed those experiences.

2. **The Situation**: This involves identifying neutral events, present factors, and the environment and understanding their impact on your existing state. Recognising that every situation itself is neutral helps us understand our personal triggers and how they affect us. The situation, together with the Existing State, is what I call the Catalyst Stack. These are the things that can change what happens next from one extreme to another.
3. **The Reaction**: Your instinctive reaction is often affected by how safe you feel and your awareness of where you sit on the spectrum of the BE elements. Reactions are immediate and driven by our emotional and physiological state. They are often automatic and can be influenced by past experiences and learned behaviours.
4. **The Response**: Unlike reactions, responses are conscious choices. With practise and self-awareness, our reactions can become more measured and deliberate responses. This shift allows us to handle situations more effectively and thoughtfully, rather than being driven purely by instinct or emotion.
5. **The New Belief**: This stage involves the habits, behaviours, and new experiences that emerge from the outcome of a situation. It reflects how we internalise and learn from our experiences, shaping our future reactions and responses. New beliefs are formed based on how we process and interpret our experiences.

Understanding and navigating the Experience Loop helps you recognise the influence of past experiences on your current emotional dynamics. It provides a structured approach to emotional regulation, enabling you to manage triggers, respond thoughtfully, and cultivate adaptive beliefs.

Think about this:

Every time you react with negative emotions or behaviour, what your mind is really stating is:

"I don't know how to process this yet, so I'm going to react with emotions or behaviour or turn this onto you to protect myself. What I'm really trying to say is that something doesn't make sense to me, and I need time to process it, or a different perspective, and I don't know how to convey that, yet."

Consider a situation or habit that no longer affects you emotionally or reactively. It's the same event happening as when it did affect you, but now you know how to process it, so there is no more reaction—only a response. When that event occurs, you handle it without getting upset. This demonstrates your growth and ability to process the situation effectively.

If there is no button to push, there will be no reaction. "Being" is allowing yourself to make your buttons harder to push, or remove them altogether. Negative emotions are not inherently bad; they are warning signs that something is not quite right and need to be addressed to prevent ongoing distress.

REMEMBER: This book focuses on emotional regulation in our normal everyday lives, not severe trauma, loss from death, or other extreme situations. What is in here can be used to process these events however it is approached from a different perspective.

The Experience Loop, with its stages of Existing State, The Situation, The Reaction, The Response, and The New Belief, provides a comprehensive framework for understanding how our behaviours and emotional responses develop and evolve. By recognising the influence of past experiences and actively engaging in the process of self-awareness and emotional regulation, we can transform our reactions into thoughtful responses and foster new, adaptive beliefs that support our overall well-being. Embrace this journey of self-discovery and growth, and remember that each step you take brings you closer to living a life of true BE-ing.

CHAPTER 10 - THE EXISTING STATE

INTRODUCTION TO THE EXISTING STATE

EVERY JOURNEY BEGINS from a starting point, a moment in time where all our past experiences, beliefs, values, and emotions converge. This is our existing state. Understanding our existing state sets the stage for how we interpret and respond to the world around us. It is the sum total of our life's experiences up to this very moment, a snapshot of our internal and external landscapes.

Assessing the Catalyst Stack

To truly understand our existing state, we need to assess the various components that comprise it. This is where the Catalyst Stack comes in —a comprehensive evaluation of our emotional, mental, and physical states, alongside our beliefs, values, legacy behaviours, cultural influences, and the events of our daily lives.

Emotional State

Our emotions are powerful drivers of our behaviour. They colour our perception of reality and influence how we respond to situations. Reflecting on our emotional state involves asking questions like: How am I feeling right now? What emotions are most prominent in my life? Am I harboring unresolved feelings from past experiences?

Mental State

Our thoughts and mental processes play a significant role in shaping our existing state. This includes our cognitive patterns, mental health, and overall mindset. Self-reflection questions might include: What recurring thoughts do I have? How do I perceive challenges? Am I optimistic or pessimistic about the future?

Physical State

Our physical well-being affects our overall state significantly. This encompasses our health, fitness, energy levels, and how we physically feel on a day-to-day basis. Consider questions like: How is my physical health? Do I feel energetic or lethargic? How do my physical sensations influence my emotions and thoughts?

Beliefs and Values

Our beliefs and values form the core of our identity. They guide our decisions and shape our understanding of the world. Reflect on: What are my core beliefs? How do my values influence my actions? Are there any beliefs that no longer serve me?

Legacy Behaviours

Legacy behaviours are ingrained patterns of behaviour passed down through generations or developed over time. These behaviours can be beneficial or detrimental. Ask yourself: What habitual behaviours do I exhibit? Are these behaviours aligned with my current values and goals?

CULTURAL AND GENERATIONAL INFLUENCES

Our cultural background and generational influences significantly shape our existing state. These influences dictate norms, expectations, and behaviours that we might unconsciously adopt. Reflect on: How has my cultural background shaped my worldview? What generational beliefs and behaviours have I inherited?

Recent Events

Daily experiences and recent events also impact our existing state. They can trigger emotions, thoughts, and behaviours that contribute to our overall state. Consider: What significant events have occurred recently? How have they affected my emotional, mental, and physical state?

> ***Where you are today is a direct reflection of your ability or inability to process every situation, shift or external influence you've ever experienced. Nothing more, nothing less.***
>
> NOLAN COLLINS

This underscores the importance of processing our experiences. Our existing state is a reflection of how we have navigated life's challenges and opportunities. Each situation, whether positive or negative, contributes to our current state based on how we process and integrate it. This emphasises the power of self-awareness and the need to continuously refine our ability to process experiences.

CAUSE AND EFFECT

Every situation we encounter is inherently neutral. The emotions and outcomes we experience depend on our ability to process what is happening. This perspective highlights the subjective nature of our experiences. Two people can face the same situation, yet their reactions and emotional outcomes can be wildly different based on their processing abilities.

For example, consider two individuals experiencing job loss. One might see it as a devastating blow to their identity and self-worth, leading to depression and anxiety. The other might view it as an opportunity for growth and exploration, leading to excitement and new beginnings. The situation itself is neutral; it is the individual's processing that defines the emotional and behavioural outcome.

CASE STUDIES: VARYING REACTIONS TO THE SAME SITUATION

To illustrate the concept of cause and effect in our existing state, let's explore a few case studies:

Receiving Constructive Criticism at Work: Two employees receive the same constructive feedback from their manager. One might react defensively, feeling attacked and undervalued, which could lead to decreased motivation and performance. The other might see the feedback as an opportunity for growth, using it to improve their skills and performance. The different outcomes arise from how each individual processes and integrates the feedback into their sense of self and professional development.

Public Speaking Engagement: When asked to present in front of a large audience, one person might experience severe anxiety and fear, potentially leading to avoidance or a subpar performance. Another person might feel excited and energised by the opportunity to share their ideas, leading to a confident and engaging presentation. These varying reactions are based on each individual's past experiences with public speaking, their current self-confidence, and their ability to regulate their emotions.

Starting a New Exercise Routine: Two friends decide to start a new exercise program together. One might feel overwhelmed by the new routine, struggling with self-doubt and giving up quickly. The other might feel motivated and invigorated, enjoying the challenge and sticking with the routine. The difference in their reactions can be attributed to their previous experiences with exercise, their current physical state, and their mindset towards personal growth and resilience.

Understanding our existing state through the Catalyst Stack allows us to gain a holistic view of our current position in life. It empowers us to see how our past experiences, beliefs, values, and recent events shape our present reality. As hard as it may seem at times, by recognising the neutrality of situations and focusing on our processing abilities, we can better navigate life's challenges and cultivate a more balanced and fulfilling life.

SELF-REFLECTION QUESTIONS FOR EXISTING STATE

Emotional State:

- What are the dominant emotions I am experiencing right now, and how do they affect my overall state?
- Are there any unresolved feelings from past experiences that are influencing my current emotional state?

Mental State:

- What recurring thoughts do I notice, and how do they impact my perception of myself and my surroundings?
- Do I tend to view challenges optimistically or pessimistically, and how does this mindset shape my reactions?

Physical State:

- How is my physical health and energy level currently, and how do these factors affect my mood and behaviour?
- What steps can I take to improve or maintain my physical well-being to better support my overall state?

Beliefs and Values:

- What are my core beliefs and values, and how do they influence my daily decisions and actions?

- Are there any beliefs I hold that no longer serve me, and how can I begin to challenge and change them?

Legacy Behaviours:

- What habitual behaviours do I exhibit, and where did they originate (e.g., family, culture, past experiences)?
- Do these legacy behaviours align with my current values and goals, or do they need to be adjusted?

Cultural and Generational Influences:

- How has my cultural background shaped my worldview and behaviours?
- What generational beliefs or practises have I inherited, and how do they influence my current state?

Recent Events:

- What significant events have occurred recently in my life, and how have they impacted my emotional, mental, and physical state?
- How do I typically process and integrate recent experiences into my overall state of being?

Overall Catalyst Stack:

- When assessing my Catalyst Stack, which element (emotional, mental, physical, beliefs, values, behaviours, cultural influences, recent events) stands out as needing the most attention?
- How can I address this element to create a more balanced and harmonious existing state?

Cause and Effect Understanding:

- In what ways do I see situations as neutral, and how does this perspective help or hinder my responses?
- How can I improve my ability to see neutrality in situations and focus on my processing skills to determine the emotional and behavioural outcomes?

CHAPTER 11 - THE SITUATION

UNDERSTANDING NEUTRALITY AND STIMULUS

EVERY DAY, we encounter countless situations that demand our attention and reaction. These situations, or stimuli, are inherently neutral. They do not possess intrinsic meaning or emotional charge. Instead, the significance and emotional impact of a situation are determined by our perceptions and interpretations. Understanding this neutrality is an important factor in learning how to navigate life's experiences more effectively.

The Concept of Situational Neutrality

Situational neutrality means that events themselves are neither good nor bad. They simply are. Two people can experience the same event but have completely different interpretations and emotional responses based on their unique perspectives and processing abilities. For example, a rainy day might be seen as a gloomy inconvenience by one person and a refreshing, nourishing event by another. The rain is neutral; it is the individual's perception that gives it meaning.

The Role of Perception in Situational Interpretation

Our perceptions are shaped by our beliefs, past experiences, emotional states, and mental frameworks. When we encounter a situation, our brain quickly processes it through these filters, assigning meaning and emotional significance. This process is often automatic and unconscious, but with practise, we can become more aware of it and learn to shift our perceptions.

Activating the Four BE Elements with the Catalyst Stack

To better understand and manage our reactions to various situations, we can use the Four BE Elements—Body, Emotions, Mind, and Spirit —alongside the Catalyst Stack. This integrated approach helps us assess and respond to stimuli more effectively.

Body

Our physical state can significantly influence how we perceive and react to situations. When we are physically well, rested, and energetic, we are more likely to handle challenges with resilience and clarity. Conversely, when we are tired, ill, or stressed, even minor issues can seem overwhelming. Regular physical self-care, including exercise, nutrition, and rest, is essential for maintaining a balanced and responsive state.

Self-Reflection Questions:

- How does my physical state influence my perception of situations?
- What can I do to maintain a healthy and balanced physical state?

Emotions

Our emotional state acts as a lens through which we view and interpret situations. Positive emotions like joy, contentment, and gratitude can enhance our ability to see the good in situations and respond constructively. Negative emotions like anger, fear, and sadness can cloud our judgment and lead to reactive behaviours. Developing emotional awareness and regulation skills is key to managing our responses effectively.

Self-Reflection Questions:

- How do my emotions shape my interpretation of events?
- What practises can I adopt to regulate my emotions better?

Mind

Our thoughts and cognitive patterns play a pivotal role in situational interpretation. A mind cluttered with negative self-talk, limiting beliefs, and cognitive distortions can skew our perception of reality. Conversely, a clear and focused mind allows us to process situations more objectively and make reasoned decisions. Mindfulness, cognitive restructuring, and mental clarity exercises can help improve our mental state.

Self-Reflection Questions:

- What thought patterns influence my interpretation of situations?
- How can I cultivate a clearer and more positive mindset?

Spirit

Our spiritual beliefs and sense of purpose provide a deeper context for interpreting situations. When we are connected to a higher purpose or meaning, we can view challenges as opportunities for growth and transformation. Spiritual practises, such as meditation, prayer, or spending time in nature, can strengthen our spiritual well-being and enhance our resilience.

Self-Reflection Questions:

- How does my spiritual perspective influence my interpretation of situations?

- What spiritual practises help me stay grounded and connected?

APPLYING THE CATALYST STACK

The Catalyst Stack—comprising our emotional, mental, and physical states, alongside our beliefs, values, legacy behaviours, cultural influences, and recent events—provides a comprehensive framework for assessing our responses to situations. By evaluating each element of the Catalyst Stack, we can gain a holistic understanding of how we interpret and react to stimuli.

Self-Reflection Questions:

- How do my beliefs and values influence my interpretation of situations?
- What cultural or generational influences shape my perceptions?
- How do recent events affect my current state and reactions?

PRACTICAL EXAMPLES OF ACTIVATING BE ELEMENTS

Example 1: Receiving Criticism at Work

Body: If I am well-rested and healthy, I am more likely to handle criticism constructively. If I am tired or unwell, I may react defensively.

Emotions: If I am feeling confident and positive, I can view criticism as helpful feedback. If I am feeling insecure or stressed, I may take it personally.

Mind: A clear and focused mind allows me to objectively evaluate the criticism and determine its validity. Negative thought patterns may lead me to dismiss it or overreact.

Spirit: A strong sense of purpose helps me see criticism as an opportunity for growth. Without this, I may struggle to find meaning in the feedback.

EXAMPLE 2: **Facing a Traffic Jam**

Body: If I am physically comfortable, I can remain patient. If I am in discomfort, my frustration may increase.

Emotions: If I am in a good mood, I might use the time to relax or listen to music. If I am already stressed, the traffic jam can escalate my anxiety.

Mind: A calm mind helps me navigate the situation without agitation. Negative thoughts can amplify my frustration.

Spirit: Seeing the delay as a chance to practise patience and mindfulness can transform the experience. Without this perspective, I may feel resentful.

Understanding the neutrality of situations and the role of our perceptions in interpreting them empowers us to respond more effectively. By activating the Four BE Elements and applying the Catalyst Stack, we can gain deeper insights into our reactions and develop healthier, more adaptive responses. In the next chapter, we will dive into the various reactions we have to situations and explore how to manage them constructively.

SELF-REFLECTION QUESTIONS FOR THE SITUATION

Understanding Neutrality:

- How do I typically perceive situations—as neutral events or as inherently positive or negative?
- What factors influence my perception of a situation's neutrality?

Role of Perception:

- How do my past experiences shape my perception of current situations?
- In what ways do my current emotional and mental states affect how I interpret events?

Body:

- How does my physical health and energy level impact my perception and reaction to daily situations?
- What physical practises can I incorporate to help me remain calm and balanced in various situations?

Emotions:

- How do my emotions colour my interpretation of neutral events?
- What techniques can I use to regulate my emotions before reacting to a situation?

Mind:

- How do my thought patterns and cognitive processes influence my perception of situations?
- What mental exercises can help me maintain a clear and objective mindset?

Spirit:

- How does my sense of purpose or spiritual beliefs affect how I view and respond to situations?
- What spiritual practises help me stay grounded and see situations more clearly?

Recent Events:

- How have recent significant events in my life affected my current emotional, mental, and physical state?
- How do I typically process and integrate recent experiences into my overall state of being?

Cause and Effect:

- How do I differentiate between the cause and effect elements in my life experiences?
- What steps can I take to focus more on my processing abilities rather than the situations themselves?

Neutrality of Situations:

- How can I practise seeing situations as neutral and focus on my responses to them?
- What examples from my life demonstrate the impact of perception on situational outcomes?

CHAPTER 12 - THE REACTION

OUR REACTIONS to situations are the outward expressions of our internal states. These reactions can manifest in various ways, ranging from snapping and withdrawing to engaging and displaying avoidant or aggressive behaviours. Understanding these behavioural outcomes helps in managing our responses and fostering healthier interactions.

IDENTIFYING COMMON REACTIONS

Snapping: This immediate, often harsh reaction can stem from stress, frustration, or feeling overwhelmed. It's a defensive response that aims to protect ourselves from perceived threats.

Withdrawing: This reaction involves retreating from the situation, either emotionally or physically. It's a way to avoid conflict or further stress but can lead to isolation and unresolved issues.

Engaging: This proactive approach involves addressing the situation head-on, seeking solutions, and communicating openly. It's a constructive reaction that promotes resolution and growth.

Avoidant Behaviour: Avoidance can manifest as procrastination, denial, or shifting focus away from the issue. While it provides temporary relief, it often exacerbates the problem in the long run.

Aggressive Behaviour: Aggression can be verbal or physical and is usually a response to perceived threats or frustration. It's a destructive reaction that can harm relationships and escalate conflicts.

THE INFLUENCE OF BE ELEMENTS ON REACTIONS

The Four BE Elements—Body, Emotions, Mind, and Spirit—play a significant role in shaping our reactions. By understanding and harnessing these elements, we can cultivate healthier and more adaptive responses.

Body

Our physical state directly impacts our reactions. When we are well-rested, healthy, and energetic, we are better equipped to handle stress and respond constructively. Conversely, physical discomfort or fatigue can lead to irritability and impulsive reactions.

Self-Reflection Questions:

How does my physical health influence my reactions?

What physical self-care practises can I implement to improve my responses?

Emotions

Our emotional state acts as a powerful driver of our reactions. Emotions like anger, fear, and sadness can trigger defensive or aggressive behaviours, while feelings of calm and contentment promote constructive engagement.

Self-Reflection Questions:

What emotions typically drive my reactions?

How can I develop better emotional regulation to improve my responses?

Mind

Our thoughts and cognitive processes shape our perceptions and, consequently, our reactions. A clear and focused mind enables us to evaluate situations objectively and respond thoughtfully, while negative thought patterns can lead to reactive and impulsive behaviours.

Self-Reflection Questions:

How do my thought patterns influence my reactions?

What mental exercises can help me cultivate a clearer and more positive mindset?

Spirit

Our spiritual beliefs and sense of purpose provide a deeper context for our reactions. A strong connection to our values and higher purpose can guide us to respond with integrity and compassion, even in challenging situations.

Self-Reflection Questions:

How does my spiritual perspective influence my reactions?

What spiritual practises help me stay grounded and responsive?

PRACTICAL EXAMPLES OF BE ELEMENTS INFLUENCING REACTIONS

Example 1: Handling Criticism at Work

Body: If I am physically comfortable and energetic, I can handle criticism with composure and openness. Physical discomfort might lead to defensive snapping.

Emotions: If I feel confident and valued, I can see criticism as constructive. If I feel insecure, I might react defensively or withdraw.

Mind: A clear mind helps me evaluate the criticism objectively. Negative thought patterns might lead me to dismiss the feedback or overreact.

Spirit: Viewing criticism as an opportunity for growth aligns with my values and purpose, helping me respond constructively. Without this perspective, I might feel threatened and react aggressively.

EXAMPLE 2: **Dealing with a Family Argument**

Body: If I am well-rested and calm, I can engage in the argument constructively. Physical exhaustion might lead to snapping or withdrawing.

Emotions: Feeling loved and secure helps me approach the argument with empathy. Feeling stressed or undervalued might trigger avoidant or aggressive behaviour.

Mind: A focused mind allows me to listen and respond thoughtfully. Negative thought patterns might lead to reactive and impulsive responses.

Spirit: Seeing the argument as a chance to strengthen family bonds guides me to engage with compassion. Without this view, I might react defensively.

STRATEGIES TO HARNESS BE ELEMENTS FOR POSITIVE REACTIONS

Mindfulness and Meditation: Practicing mindfulness helps cultivate awareness of our thoughts and emotions, enabling us to respond rather than react impulsively.

Physical Self-Care: Regular exercise, a balanced diet, and adequate sleep improve our physical state, enhancing our ability to handle stress.

Emotional Regulation Techniques: Techniques such as deep breathing, journaling, and seeking social support help manage emotions effectively.

Cognitive Restructuring: Challenging negative thought patterns and reframing them positively promotes clearer and more constructive thinking.

Spiritual practises: Engaging in spiritual practises that resonate with us, such as prayer, meditation, or spending time in nature, helps maintain a sense of purpose and grounding.

SELF-REFLECTION QUESTIONS FOR THE REACTION

Body:

- How does my physical state influence my reactions to challenging situations?
- What physical self-care practises can I implement to improve my ability to handle stress?

Emotions:

- What emotions typically drive my reactions, and how do they impact my behaviour?
- How can I develop better emotional regulation to respond more constructively?

Mind:

- How do my thought patterns influence my reactions to various situations?
- What mental exercises can help me cultivate a clearer and more positive mindset?

Spirit:

- How does my spiritual perspective influence my reactions to difficult situations?
- What spiritual practises help me stay grounded and responsive in the face of challenges?

Behavioural Outcomes:

- What common reactions do I exhibit when faced with stress or conflict (e.g., snapping, withdrawing, engaging)?
- How can I become more aware of these reactions and work towards more constructive responses?

Influence of BE Elements:

- How do the Four BE Elements (Body, Emotions, Mind, Spirit) individually and collectively shape my reactions?
- What steps can I take to balance these elements and improve my overall response to situations?

Criticism at Work:

- How do I typically react to criticism at work, and what drives these reactions?
- What changes can I make to handle criticism more constructively?

Family Arguments:

- How do I usually respond to family arguments, and what influences these responses?
- What strategies can I adopt to engage in family conflicts with more empathy and understanding?

Managing Stress:

- How do stress and physical discomfort affect my reactions to daily challenges?
- What practises can I incorporate to manage stress and maintain a calm demeanour?

Constructive Engagement:

- How can I cultivate the habit of engaging constructively in difficult situations rather than reacting impulsively?
- What role do my values and sense of purpose play in shaping my reactions?

CHAPTER 13 - THE RESPONSE

INTERNAL VS. EXTERNAL FEEDBACK

OUR RESPONSES to situations are shaped by both internal and external feedback. Internal feedback involves self-reflection and self-assessment, while external feedback comes from the reactions and inputs of others.

Internal Feedback: Self-Reflection and Self-Assessment

Internal feedback is the process of looking inward to evaluate our thoughts, emotions, and behaviours. This self-reflection allows us to gain insight into why we responded a certain way and what we can learn from the experience. It involves asking ourselves questions, creating a sense of safety, seeking clarity, and tuning into our deeper selves to make deliberate choices.

Self-Reflection Questions:

- How do I typically reflect on my responses to situations?
- What internal dialogue do I engage in after reacting to an event?

- How can I improve my self-assessment skills to foster growth?

External Feedback: Reactions and Inputs from Others

External feedback is the information we receive from others about our behaviours and responses. This feedback can provide valuable perspectives and help us see things we might miss in our self-assessment. It can come from friends, family, colleagues, or even strangers.

Self-Reflection Questions:

- How open am I to receiving feedback from others?
- How do I typically react to constructive criticism?
- What steps can I take to seek and incorporate external feedback more effectively?

Forming, Adapting, and Solidifying Beliefs

Our responses to situations contribute to the formation and adaptation of our beliefs. By reflecting on our experiences and the feedback we receive, we can adapt our beliefs to align with our values and goals. Over time, these beliefs solidify, becoming integral parts of our identity.

Self-Reflection Questions:

- How do my responses to situations shape my beliefs?
- What beliefs have I formed based on past experiences?
- How can I adapt my beliefs to better serve my current goals and values?

Conscious Response vs. Instinctive Reaction

As noted earlier, "every situational emotional reaction is our brain telling us we don't know how to process the situation." This quote highlights the importance of moving from an instinctive reaction to a conscious response. Instead of reacting impulsively, we take the time to understand the situation, ask questions, create safety, seek clarity, and make deliberate choices.

Implementing a Conscious Response

Assess the Situation: Take a moment to pause and observe the situation without immediate judgment. Understand that the initial emotional reaction is an indication of the need for deeper processing.

Create Safety: Ensure that you feel emotionally and physically safe before responding. This might involve stepping back from the situation temporarily, taking deep breaths, or finding a calm space.

Seek Clarity: Ask yourself and others clarifying questions to fully understand the context and details of the situation. Clarity reduces uncertainty and helps in making informed decisions.

Tune into Yourself: Reflect on your thoughts, emotions, and physical sensations. Understanding your internal state helps in aligning your response with your true self.

Engage in the Conversation: Consciously choose to contribute to the conversation or situation in a way that is constructive and aligned with your values. This might involve expressing your thoughts calmly, asking for more information, or suggesting solutions.

EXAMPLE: **Handling Conflict at Work**

Assess the Situation: Pause to understand the nature of the conflict and the perspectives involved.

Create Safety: Take a few deep breaths to calm down and ensure you feel safe to engage.

Seek Clarity: Ask clarifying questions to understand the root cause of the conflict.

Tune into Yourself: Reflect on your own feelings and thoughts about the conflict.

Engage in the Conversation: Respond calmly and constructively, focusing on finding a resolution.

EXAMPLE: **Dealing with Personal Disappointment**

Assess the Situation: Identify the cause of the disappointment and its impact on you.

Create Safety: Find a quiet place to reflect and ensure you feel safe to process your emotions.

Seek Clarity: Understand what led to the disappointment and what expectations were not met.

Tune into Yourself: Reflect on your emotional and mental state.

Engage in the Conversation: Decide how to address the disappointment constructively, whether it involves speaking to someone or making a personal change.

A BRIEF INTRODUCTION TO RAMP-IT

In The Experience Loop, the Response is where our understanding of self-coaching and choosing how we want to move forward coincides with the RAMPIT Framework. You have a few chapters coming up that break down the RAMPIT Framework, however, to give it context here, I've added a very brief overview of the framework.

The RAMP-IT framework guides us in managing our responses and forming healthy outcomes. It stands for Purposeful, Mind/Body State, Accountable, Resourceful, Influential, and True. By following these principles, we can ensure that our responses lead to positive growth and well-being.

Purposeful: Aligning actions with a clear purpose and intent and understanding of who we need to be.

Mind/Body State: Maintaining a balanced and healthy mental and physical state.

Accountable: Taking responsibility for our actions and their outcomes.

Resourceful: Using available resources effectively to handle situations.

Influential: Positively influencing ourselves and others through our responses.

True: Staying authentic and true to our values and beliefs.

EXAMPLE: **Handling Conflict at Work Using RAMP-IT**

Purposeful: Align my approach to conflict with my goal of fostering a collaborative work environment.

Mind/Body State: Ensure I am well-rested and calm before engaging in conflict resolution.

Accountable: Take responsibility for my role in the conflict and its resolution.

Resourceful: Use available conflict resolution tools and seek advice if needed.

Influential: Aim to influence the situation positively by promoting understanding and compromise.

True: Stay true to my values of respect and honesty throughout the process.

EXAMPLE: **Coping with Personal Loss Using RAMP-IT**

Purposeful: Find meaning and purpose in the grieving process, such as honouring the memory of the person you're grieving.

Mind/Body State: Prioritise self-care to maintain physical and mental health during the grieving process.

Accountable: Accept and process my emotions, taking responsibility for my healing journey.

Resourceful: Use support systems, such as friends, family, or grief counselling.

Influential: Share my experience to help others going through similar losses.

True: Allow myself to feel and express my true emotions without suppression.

SELF-REFLECTION QUESTIONS FOR THE RESPONSE

Internal Feedback:

- How do I typically reflect on my responses to situations?
- What internal dialogue do I engage in after reacting to an event?
- How can I improve my self-assessment skills to foster growth?

External Feedback:

- How open am I to receiving feedback from others?
- How do I typically react to constructive criticism?
- What steps can I take to seek and incorporate external feedback more effectively?

Conscious Response:

- How can I shift from instinctive reactions to conscious responses?

- What steps can I take to ensure I respond deliberately rather than impulsively?

Assessing the Situation:

- How do I take the time to assess situations before responding?
- What techniques help me pause and reflect before reacting?

Creating Safety:

- How do I create a sense of safety for myself before responding to challenging situations?
- What practises help me feel emotionally and physically safe?

Seeking Clarity:

- How can I seek clarity in confusing or ambiguous situations?
- What questions can I ask to better understand the context and details?

Tuning into Myself:

- How do I tune into my thoughts, emotions, and physical sensations before responding?
- What practises help me connect with my deeper self?

Engaging in the Conversation:

- How can I consciously choose to contribute constructively to conversations and situations?
- What strategies help me express my thoughts and feelings calmly and clearly?

CHAPTER 14 - THE NEW BELIEF

INCORPORATING NEW BELIEFS INTO IDENTITY

BELIEFS ARE the lens through which we view the world, influencing our thoughts, emotions, and actions. As we go through life, our experiences and reflections can lead us to form new beliefs. Incorporating these new beliefs into our identity is a transformative process that requires intentionality and openness.

Understanding the Process of Belief Formation

Belief formation is an ongoing process influenced by our experiences, reflections, and feedback from the environment. When we encounter new information or perspectives, we may need to reassess and modify our existing beliefs. This adaptability is essential for personal growth and resilience.

Self-Reflection Questions:

- What new beliefs have I formed recently, and why?
- How do these new beliefs align with my core values and goals?

- What old beliefs no longer serve me, and how can I let them go?

STRATEGIES FOR INTEGRATING NEW BELIEFS

Reflect on the Belief: Take time to deeply understand the new belief and its implications for your life. Reflect on how it aligns with your values and goals.

Challenge Old Beliefs: Identify any old beliefs that conflict with the new one. Reflect on why they no longer serve you and consciously decide to release them.

practise Affirmations: Regularly practise affirmations to reinforce the new belief and solidify it in your subconscious mind.

Align Actions with Beliefs: Ensure that your daily actions reflect the new belief. Consistent actions aligned with your beliefs help in integrating them into your identity.

Seek Support: Share your new beliefs with supportive friends or mentors. Their encouragement and feedback can reinforce your commitment to the new belief.

EXAMPLE: **Embracing a Growth Mindset**

Reflect on the Belief: Understand that intelligence and abilities can be developed through effort and learning.

Challenge Old Beliefs: Let go of the fixed mindset that views abilities as static and unchangeable.

practise Affirmations: Regularly affirm, "I am capable of growing and improving through effort and learning."

Align Actions with Beliefs: Engage in new learning opportunities and embrace challenges.

Seek Support: Share your growth mindset journey with a mentor who encourages continuous learning.

Preparing for Future Shifts

Life is dynamic, and our beliefs may need to adapt to new circumstances and information. Being prepared for future shifts involves maintaining flexibility and openness.

Self-Reflection Questions:

- How can I stay open to new information and perspectives?
- What practises help me remain adaptable and resilient in the face of change?
- How can I balance holding on to core values while being open to modifying my beliefs?

Continuous Growth and Evolution

Personal growth is a lifelong journey. By continuously reflecting on and adapting our beliefs, we can evolve and thrive. This process involves staying curious, embracing change, and committing to self-improvement.

Self-Reflection Questions:

- What areas of my life would benefit from new beliefs or perspectives?
- How can I foster a mindset of continuous growth and learning?
- What steps can I take to ensure that my beliefs evolve with my experiences and knowledge?

MORE SELF-REFLECTION QUESTIONS FOR THE NEW BELIEF

Understanding Belief Formation:

- What new beliefs have I formed recently, and why?
- How do these new beliefs align with my core values and goals?
- What old beliefs no longer serve me, and how can I let them go?

Reflecting on New Beliefs:

- How does this new belief impact my daily life and decisions?
- In what ways can I deepen my understanding of this new belief?

Challenging Old Beliefs:

- What old beliefs conflict with this new belief, and why do they no longer serve me?
- How can I consciously release these outdated beliefs?

Practising Affirmations:

- What affirmations can I use to reinforce my new belief?
- How can I incorporate these affirmations into my daily routine?

Aligning Actions with Beliefs:

- How can I ensure that my actions reflect my new belief?
- What specific steps can I take to live out this belief in my daily life?

Seeking Support:

- Who can I share my new beliefs with to receive support and encouragement?

- How can I engage with supportive communities that align with my new beliefs?

Preparing for Future Shifts:

- How can I stay open to new information and perspectives?
- What practises help me remain adaptable and resilient in the face of change?

Continuous Growth and Evolution:

- What areas of my life would benefit from new beliefs or perspectives?
- How can I foster a mindset of continuous growth and learning?

Balancing Core Values with Adaptability:

- How can I balance holding on to core values while being open to modifying my beliefs?
- What steps can I take to ensure that my beliefs evolve with my experiences and knowledge?

Practical Applications:

- How can I apply the concepts of belief integration and adaptability in my daily life?
- What specific actions can I take to maintain a balanced and fulfilling existence?

PART FOUR

CHAPTER 15 - KEEP MOVING FORWARDS - AN INTRODUCTION TO THE RAMP-IT FRAMEWORK

We've covered a lot so far, and this next section is really about how to self-coach with a framework that covers the important factors that help make successful situations successful!

Take a break, stand up, take a few deep breaths, relax your shoulders, and grab a glass of water. This part contains a lot to think about too.

I uncovered this framework when teaching apprentices, by sending out regular emails to help them be more Accountable, use the Resources available, check in with their own Mind/Body state, keep the Purpose of what they were doing in mind, share and be Influential to others, and be True, or honest with themselves.

If you were paying attention, you'll notice the acronym started as ARMPIT. I realise that would not be a good acronym for personal development so moved the R to the front! Now it works!

The RAMP-IT Framework is a comprehensive approach designed to enhance self-coaching, personal growth, and emotional regulation. By integrating these factors into our daily lives, we can navigate challenges more effectively, achieve our goals, and cultivate a sense of calm and presence. The RAMP-IT factors provide a structured methodology to guide our actions, decisions, and interactions, enabling us to live more intentionally and authentically.

THE RAMP-IT FRAMEWORK CONSISTS OF SIX MAIN FACTORS:

Purposeful: This factor emphasises acting with intention and understanding the broader purpose behind our actions. It involves recognising our role in various situations, clarifying our intent, identifying the cause we are supporting, and understanding how our actions serve others. Being purposeful helps us stay aligned with our values and long-term goals, providing a sense of direction and meaning in our lives.

Mind/Body Awareness: This factor focuses on integrating mental and physical well-being. It involves creating a supportive environment, accepting our current state, recognising physical sensations, managing our thoughts, and regulating our emotions. Maintaining a balanced mind/body state is an important consideration for overall health and resilience, allowing us to respond to challenges with clarity and composure.

Accountable: Being accountable means taking responsibility for our actions and decisions. This factor involves understanding the situation, establishing processes, setting expectations, anticipating challenges, and regularly reviewing progress. Accountability fosters a sense of ownership and commitment, ensuring that we follow through on our intentions and learn from our experiences.

Resourceful: This factor is about effectively using available resources to achieve our goals. It involves leveraging knowledge, individuals, tools, and external sources to support our efforts. Being resourceful helps us overcome obstacles and find creative solutions, enhancing our ability to adapt and thrive in various situations.

Influential: This factor emphasises the positive impact we can have on others. It involves leading by example, communicating effectively, showing genuine interest in others, and sharing experiences. Being influential helps us build strong relationships, inspire positive change, and create a supportive community around us.

True: This factor is about living authentically and sincerely. It involves embracing vulnerability, staying true to our values, and maintaining transparency in our actions. Being true to ourselves fosters trust and integrity, allowing us to build deeper connections and live a life that reflects our true identity and beliefs.

WHY THE RAMP-IT FACTORS ARE IMPORTANT

Understanding and integrating the RAMP-IT factors into our daily lives is essential for several reasons:

Clarity and Focus: The RAMP-IT factors provide a clear framework to guide our actions and decisions. By being purposeful and accountable, we can set clear goals and stay focused on achieving them. This clarity helps us navigate challenges with a sense of direction and purpose.

Emotional Regulation: Maintaining a balanced mind/body state and being true to ourselves helps us regulate our emotions more effectively. This regulation is key for managing stress, overcoming setbacks, and responding thoughtfully to situations, rather than reacting impulsively.

Personal Growth: The RAMP-IT factors encourage continuous learning and self-improvement. By being resourceful and accountable, we can leverage our experiences to grow and develop, enhancing our skills and abilities over time.

Building Relationships: Being influential and true to ourselves fosters strong, supportive relationships. Effective communication, genuine interest, and integrity help us build trust and collaboration, creating a positive and empowering environment.

Resilience and Adaptability: The RAMP-IT factors equip us with the tools and mindset needed to adapt to change and overcome challenges.

By being resourceful and maintaining a balanced mind/body state, we can navigate uncertainty with confidence and resilience.

Authentic Living: Ultimately, the RAMP-IT factors help us live more authentically and meaningfully. By aligning our actions with our values and purpose, we can create a life that reflects our true identity and aspirations, fostering a deep sense of fulfillment and well-being.

CHAPTER 16 - PURPOSEFUL

UNDERSTANDING ROLE

UNDERSTANDING your role in any given situation is key to acting with purpose. Roles are the various hats we wear in life, each bringing its own set of responsibilities, expectations, and opportunities for growth. Whether you are at work, home, or within a social setting, recognising and embracing your role can help you navigate interactions with clarity and intention.

Defining Roles and Responsibilities

Roles are not static; they shift and evolve based on the context and the relationships involved. For example, you might be a manager at work, a parent at home, a mentor in your community, or a friend in your social circle. Each role carries unique responsibilities and influences how you interact with others and the decisions you make.

Consider the specific responsibilities associated with each role. As a manager, your role might involve guiding your team, setting goals, and providing support. At home, as a parent, you might focus on nurturing and teaching your children. In all these roles, there is an underlying expectation that you contribute positively to the situation.

Reflect on the roles you occupy in your life. What responsibilities do you associate with each? How do these roles align with your personal values and goals? Understanding these aspects can help you navigate your roles more effectively and with greater purpose.

Role Characteristics and Self-Perception

Beyond titles, roles also encompass certain characteristics or qualities. For example, being a leader might involve traits like decisiveness, empathy, and resilience. Being a mentor might emphasise patience, knowledge-sharing, and supportiveness. These characteristics shape how you perceive yourself and how others perceive you.

It's important to recognise both the positive and negative aspects of your role characteristics. For instance, while decisiveness is crucial in a leadership role, it might also lead to burnout if not balanced with self-care.

Reflect on the characteristics you embody in your various roles. Are there traits that you need to develop further? Are there aspects you need to manage or balance better? Understanding these traits can help you align your self-perception with your actions, fostering a more authentic and effective presence in each role.

Navigating Open and Closed States

Your emotional and cognitive states also influence roles. Being in an "open" state means being receptive, flexible, and willing to engage with new ideas and perspectives. This state fosters creativity, learning, and positive interactions. Conversely, a "closed" state is characterised by defensiveness, rigidity, and resistance to change, which can limit growth and strain relationships.

Imagine a sponge—when it's squeezed tight in a fist, it cannot absorb water or release what it holds. This symbolises a closed state, where you are not receptive to feedback, new ideas or new experiences. Now, picture the sponge resting openly on a palm, ready to absorb and release. This represents an open state, where you are willing to engage, learn, and share.

Reflect on a recent situation where you felt resistant or defensive. What was the outcome? How might an open state have changed the interaction? Consider how you can shift from a closed to an open state, especially in challenging situations. This shift is crucial for personal growth and effective role fulfilment.

PRACTICAL STEPS FOR EMBRACING ROLES

Role Reflection: Regularly assess the roles you play in your life. Consider the responsibilities, expectations, and characteristics associated with each. Reflect on how these elements align with your personal values and goals.

Character Development: Identify traits that are essential for your roles. Work on developing positive characteristics and managing those that might be counterproductive. This ongoing development is key to fulfilling your roles effectively.

Mindset Awareness: Be mindful of your emotional and cognitive states. Strive to maintain an open state, especially in challenging or new situations. Use techniques like mindfulness or reflection to shift your mindset from closed to open when necessary.

Intentional Action: Align your actions with the responsibilities and characteristics of your roles. Be intentional in how you fulfill your roles, ensuring that your actions are consistent with your values and goals.

Feedback and Adjustment: Seek feedback from others and be willing to adjust your approach. This feedback can provide valuable insights into how others perceive your role and help you make necessary improvements.

Reflective Questions:

- How do my current roles align with my core values and goals?
- What characteristics do I embody in these roles, and how do they impact my interactions?
- How can I shift from a closed to an open state in my roles?
- What steps can I take to improve my effectiveness in my roles?

INTENT: ACTING WITH CLEAR PURPOSE

Acting with clear intent means knowing why you do what you do. It's about aligning your actions with your goals and values, bringing a focused and deliberate approach to your daily life. This clarity not only enhances your effectiveness but also adds meaning and direction to your efforts.

Clarifying Intentions

Intentions are like the compass that guides your actions. They ensure that what you do each day moves you closer to your goals and aligns with your core values. Without clear intentions, it's easy to get caught up in busywork that may not contribute to your overall purpose.

To clarify your intentions, start by reflecting on your primary goals. What are the key objectives you wish to achieve in your personal and professional life? Once you've identified these goals, consider how your daily actions contribute to them. Are there activities you engage in that align with these goals, or are there areas where your efforts are scattered?

Reflective Questions:

- What are my primary goals, and how do my daily actions support them?
- Are there activities that distract me from my goals, and how can I minimise them?
- How can I ensure that my intentions are aligned with my core values?

Aligning Actions with Values

Aligning your actions with your values means ensuring that what you do reflects what you believe in. This alignment is crucial for maintaining integrity and authenticity in your actions. When your actions are consistent with your values, you feel more satisfied and at peace with your decisions.

Reflect on your core values—such as honesty, compassion, growth, or resilience—and evaluate how well your actions reflect these values. For instance, if you value honesty, consider whether your interactions are transparent and sincere. If you value growth, think about how you are pushing yourself to learn and evolve.

Reflective Questions:

- What are my core values, and how do they manifest in my actions?
- Are there discrepancies between my values and actions? If so, how can I address them?
- What steps can I take to better align my actions with my values?

Setting Clear Goals

Setting clear and achievable goals is a practical way to translate your intentions into action. Goals provide direction and motivation, helping you focus your efforts on what truly matters. When setting goals, consider both short-term objectives and long-term aspirations.

Ensure that your goals are specific, measurable, achievable, relevant, and time-bound (SMART). This clarity helps you track your progress and stay accountable. Regularly reviewing your goals can also help you stay aligned with your evolving values and circumstances.

Reflective Questions:

- What are my current short-term and long-term goals?

- How can I make my goals more specific and measurable?
- How often do I review my goals, and what can I do to stay on track?

CAUSE: CONNECTING TO A LARGER MISSION

Believing in the purpose behind your actions connects your daily activities to a larger mission or vision. This sense of cause provides deeper motivation and fulfillment, as it allows you to contribute to something greater than yourself.

Identifying Your Cause

To find your cause, reflect on what issues or missions resonate with you deeply. It could be a professional goal, a personal passion, or a social issue that you care about. This cause should inspire and motivate you, giving you a sense of direction and purpose.

Once you've identified your cause, think about how you can incorporate it into your daily life. This might involve volunteering, advocating for a cause, or integrating your passion into your work or hobbies. Even small, consistent actions can build towards significant impact over time.

Reflective Questions:

- What cause or mission am I passionate about?
- How does this cause align with my values and goals?
- How can I incorporate this cause into my daily life?

Staying Committed

Staying committed to your cause requires regular reminders and reinforcement. Use visual reminders, such as vision boards or affirmations, to keep your cause front and centre in your mind. Reflect regularly on the impact of your actions and how they contribute to your cause.

Reflective Questions:

- What steps can I take to reinforce my commitment to my cause?
- How can I track the impact of my actions related to this cause?
- What challenges might arise, and how can I prepare to overcome them?

SERVICE: CONTRIBUTING POSITIVELY TO OTHERS

Service involves using your strengths to contribute positively to others while maintaining your well-being. It's about finding a balance between giving and taking care of yourself, ensuring that your contributions are sustainable and enriching.

Identifying Strengths and Setting Boundaries

Recognise the strengths you bring to your roles and how you can use them to help others. Whether it's your ability to listen, organise, lead, or empathise, these strengths can be leveraged to make a positive impact. However, it's important to set boundaries to avoid overextending yourself. Clear boundaries protect your time and energy, ensuring that your service to others does not come at the expense of your own well-being.

Reflective Questions:

- What are my key strengths, and how can I use them to help others?
- What boundaries do I need to set to ensure my well-being?
- How can I communicate these boundaries effectively?

Practicing Self-Care

Self-care is essential for sustaining your ability to serve others. It involves regularly engaging in activities that replenish your energy and promote physical, mental, and emotional well-being. This might include exercise, meditation, hobbies, or simply taking time to rest.

Reflective Questions:

- What self-care practises do I currently engage in?
- How do these practises support my overall well-being?
- Are there additional self-care activities I can incorporate into my routine?

INTEGRATING PURPOSEFUL ACTIONS INTO DAILY LIFE

To live purposefully means to continually reflect, adjust, and apply your understanding of roles, intentions, causes, and service in your daily life. This process involves regular self-assessment and a willingness to adapt as your circumstances and understanding evolve.

Reflective Questions:

- How can I create a daily routine that incorporates awareness of my role, intentions, cause, and service?
- What steps can I take to ensure I am consistently aligned with my values and goals?
- How can I integrate reflection, adjustment, and application into my daily life?

By embracing these elements, you can lead a more purposeful and fulfilling life, acting with intention and clarity. This purposeful approach not only enhances your personal growth but also positively impacts the broader community. In the next chapter, we will explore how to cultivate a balanced mind/body state, focusing on creating supportive environments, embracing acceptance, and regulating emotions for overall well-being.

CHAPTER 17 - MIND/BODY STATE - HOLISTIC WELL-BEING

HOLISTIC WELL-BEING IS the foundation of a balanced and fulfilling life. It involves recognising and nurturing the interconnectedness of our mental and physical states, and understanding how these influence our emotions, thoughts, and actions. In this chapter, we explore how to cultivate a balanced mind/body state using the SAFTE framework: Setting, Acceptance, Feelings, Thoughts, and Emotions.

SETTING

Your environment plays a crucial role in shaping your mental and emotional well-being. A supportive setting is one that fosters peace, clarity, and positivity, helping you to feel grounded and focused.

Physical Space and Mental Clarity

The physical spaces we inhabit—whether at home, work, or elsewhere—can significantly impact our mental state. Cluttered or chaotic environments can lead to feelings of stress and overwhelm, while organised, calm spaces can promote relaxation and clear thinking.

Consider your current living and working spaces. Are they conducive to a peaceful and productive mindset? Simple changes, such as decluttering, adding plants, or incorporating calming colours, can make a substantial difference in how you feel and function.

Reflective Questions:

- How does my current environment affect my mood and productivity?
- What changes can I make to create a more supportive and calming space?
- How can I maintain an organised and inviting environment?

Emotional Environment and Relationships

Just as our physical environment impacts us, so too do our emotional environments—the relationships and social interactions that surround us. Positive relationships can provide support, encouragement, and a sense of belonging, while toxic or negative relationships can drain energy and contribute to emotional distress.

Reflect on the key relationships in your life. Are they uplifting and supportive, or do they often lead to feelings of frustration and anxiety? It's important to cultivate relationships that enhance your well-being and to set boundaries with those that do not.

Reflective Questions:

- Who in my life provides positive support and encouragement?
- Are there relationships that consistently cause me stress or discomfort?
- What boundaries can I set to protect my emotional well-being?

ACCEPTANCE

Acceptance is about acknowledging reality as it is, rather than as we wish it to be. It's a crucial aspect of emotional regulation, helping us to respond to situations with calmness and clarity rather than resistance and frustration.

Acceptance of Emotions

All emotions, whether positive or negative, are a natural part of the human experience. Accepting your emotions means allowing yourself to feel them without judgment or suppression. This acceptance can reduce internal conflict and promote a healthier emotional state.

Reflect on how you typically respond to challenging emotions. Do you try to avoid or suppress them, or do you acknowledge and process them? Practising mindfulness and self-compassion can help you embrace your emotions and understand what they are trying to communicate.

Reflective Questions:

- How do I currently handle difficult emotions?
- What emotions do I find challenging to accept, and why?
- How can I practise self-compassion in moments of emotional distress?

Acceptance of Circumstances

Acceptance also extends to the external circumstances of our lives. While we cannot control everything that happens, we can control our response to it. Accepting circumstances as they are—without denial or resistance—allows us to focus our energy on constructive actions and solutions.

Reflect on a recent challenging situation. How did you react? Did you find yourself resisting the reality of the situation, or were you able to accept it and focus on what you could control? Practising acceptance doesn't mean passive resignation but rather acknowledging reality and choosing how to respond.

Reflective Questions:

- How do I respond to situations that are beyond my control?
- In what ways do I resist reality, and how does this affect me?
- What can I do to cultivate a mindset of acceptance and proactive response?

FEELINGS

Feelings are the body's response to emotions, providing valuable insights into our internal state. Recognising and understanding these feelings is essential for emotional regulation and overall well-being.

Identifying Feelings

Identifying feelings accurately is the first step in understanding and managing them. Feelings often manifest as physical sensations in the body—tightness in the chest, a fluttering stomach, or tense shoulders. Being attuned to these sensations helps you recognise when you are stressed, anxious, or calm.

Reflective Questions:

- What physical sensations do I notice when I experience different emotions?
- How can I become more aware of these sensations in real-time?
- How do these physical feelings inform my emotional state?

Managing Feelings

Once you can identify your feelings, the next step is managing them constructively. This might involve techniques such as deep breathing, progressive muscle relaxation, or simply allowing yourself to fully experience the emotion without acting on it impulsively. These practises help you maintain control and respond thoughtfully rather than reactively.

Reflective Questions:

- What techniques have I used to manage my feelings, and how effective were they?
- How can I integrate these techniques into my daily routine?
- What new methods can I explore to better manage my feelings?

THOUGHTS

Our thoughts significantly influence our emotions and actions. Understanding and managing your thought patterns is crucial for maintaining mental clarity and emotional balance.

Challenging Negative Thoughts

Negative thoughts, often automatic and deeply ingrained, can distort reality and fuel negative emotions. Challenging these thoughts involves questioning their validity and replacing them with more balanced, constructive perspectives. This process, known as cognitive restructuring, can help reduce anxiety and improve emotional well-being.

Reflective Questions:

- What negative thoughts do I frequently experience, and how do they affect me?
- How can I challenge these thoughts and replace them with more balanced perspectives?
- What impact does this cognitive shift have on my emotions and actions?

Cultivating Positive Thinking

Cultivating positive thinking doesn't mean ignoring reality or pretending everything is perfect. Instead, it's about focusing on constructive and solution-oriented thoughts that encourage resilience and optimism. Techniques such as appreciation journaling, positive affirmations, and visualisation can help shift your mindset towards positivity.

Reflective Questions:

- How often do I focus on positive aspects of my life, and how does it affect me?
- What practises can I adopt to cultivate a more positive mindset?
- How can I integrate gratitude and affirmations into my daily routine?

EMOTIONS

Emotional regulation involves managing and responding to your emotions in healthy ways. It is a critical skill for maintaining mental health and building resilience.

Understanding Emotional Triggers

Identifying your emotional triggers—specific situations, thoughts, or experiences that provoke a strong emotional response—is the first step in effective emotional regulation. Understanding these triggers allows you to anticipate and prepare for challenging emotions.

Reflect on recent instances when you experienced strong emotions. What were the triggers? How did you react, and what was the outcome? By recognising these patterns, you can begin to develop strategies to manage your responses more effectively.

Much of this book is about recognising triggers and reactive behaviour, and when self-coaching in the context of personal growth, thinking ahead to what might trigger you, or prepare to be with people who trigger you helps you be calmer in those situations.

Reflective Questions:

- What are my common emotional triggers?
- How do these triggers typically affect me?
- What strategies can I use to manage my responses to these triggers?

TECHNIQUES FOR EMOTIONAL REGULATION

There are various techniques to help regulate emotions, including mindfulness, deep breathing, and cognitive restructuring. Mindfulness involves staying present and aware of your thoughts and feelings without judgment, which can prevent you from being overwhelmed by negative emotions. Deep breathing and relaxation techniques can help calm the nervous system, reducing the physical symptoms of stress.

Reflective Questions:

- What emotional regulation techniques have I tried, and how effective were they?
- How can I incorporate mindfulness and relaxation techniques into my daily routine?
- What unhelpful thoughts do I often have, and how can I reframe them?

Building Resilience

Resilience is the ability to bounce back from adversity. It involves not only enduring challenges but also growing from them. Building resilience requires a combination of emotional regulation, a positive mindset, and supportive relationships.

Reflect on times when you have faced adversity. How did you cope, and what helped you overcome the challenges? Consider what strategies or resources you can strengthen to enhance your resilience.

Reflective Questions:

- How resilient do I feel in the face of challenges?
- What past experiences have strengthened my resilience?
- What can I do to build greater resilience in the future?

INTEGRATING MIND/BODY PRACTISES INTO DAILY LIFE

Achieving holistic well-being requires ongoing attention to both your mental and physical states. Regularly engage in practises that support your mind/body balance, such as exercise, healthy eating, adequate sleep, and stress management techniques.

Reflective Questions:

- How well do I currently manage my physical and mental well-being?
- What daily practises support my holistic health, and where can I improve?
- How can I create a balanced routine that includes physical activity, relaxation, and mental self-care?

By cultivating a balanced mind/body state, you can enhance your overall well-being, improve your emotional regulation, and build resilience. This holistic approach is essential for navigating life's challenges with grace and maintaining a fulfilling and purposeful life. In the next chapter, we will delve into the concept of accountability, exploring how taking responsibility for your actions can lead to greater self-awareness and growth.

CHAPTER 18 - ACCOUNTABLE - TAKING RESPONSIBILITY

ACCOUNTABILITY IS a critical component of personal growth and effective self-coaching. It involves taking responsibility for your actions, decisions, and their outcomes. By embracing accountability, you enhance self-awareness, build trust in relationships, and lay the groundwork for continuous improvement. This chapter explores the SPEAR framework—Situation, Processes, Expectations, Anticipate, and Review—detailing how each element contributes to a holistic approach to accountability.

SITUATION: UNDERSTANDING YOUR CONTEXT

Understanding the context or situation in which you operate is crucial for accountability. It involves recognising both external and internal factors that influence your decisions and actions. A clear understanding of your situation provides the foundation for making informed and responsible choices.

Analysing the Situation

Begin by assessing your current circumstances. What are the key elements of your situation? Consider environmental factors, relationships, available resources, and any constraints or opportunities present. Understanding these elements helps clarify what you can control and what lies beyond your control.

Reflective Questions:

- What are the key aspects of my current situation?
- How do these factors influence my actions and decisions?
- What elements of the situation can I control, and what are beyond my control?

Internal and External Influences

Understanding your situation requires recognising the internal and external influences on your behaviour. Internal influences include personal beliefs, values, and emotions, while external influences encompass societal norms, others' expectations, and environmental conditions.

Reflective Questions:

- What internal factors (beliefs, values, emotions) influence my actions?
- How do external influences (social norms, expectations) impact my decisions?
- How can I differentiate between internal and external influences when making decisions?

PROCESSES: ESTABLISHING EFFECTIVE SYSTEMS

Processes refer to the systems and routines you establish to achieve your goals. These structures are essential for maintaining consistency, managing time effectively, and ensuring that you meet your responsibilities.

Creating Effective Processes

Effective processes streamline your actions, making it easier to achieve your objectives. These processes might include planning tools, time management strategies, and regular check-ins. Well-established processes help you stay organised and focused, reducing the likelihood of errors and oversights.

Reflective Questions:

- What processes do I currently use to manage my responsibilities?
- How effective are these processes in helping me achieve my goals?
- What new processes or systems could I implement to improve efficiency?

Consistency and Adaptability

While consistency in following processes is important, adaptability is also crucial. Circumstances can change, and being flexible enough to adjust your processes when necessary ensures that you remain effective and responsive to new challenges.

Reflective Questions:

- How consistent am I in following my established processes?
- How adaptable am I when changes or challenges arise?
- How can I balance consistency with flexibility in my processes?

EXPECTATIONS: SETTING REALISTIC STANDARDS

Setting clear and realistic expectations for yourself and others is a key aspect of accountability. It involves understanding what can be reasonably achieved within a given timeframe and being transparent about what you can deliver.

Defining Expectations

Start by clearly defining what you expect from yourself and others in specific situations. This clarity helps prevent misunderstandings and sets a standard for performance and behaviour. It's important to ensure that these expectations are realistic and aligned with your capabilities and resources.

Reflective Questions:

- What expectations do I have for myself in my personal and professional roles?
- Are these expectations realistic and achievable?
- How do I communicate my expectations to others?

Managing Expectations

Managing expectations involves regularly reviewing and adjusting them as necessary. This process helps accommodate changes in circumstances or new information, ensuring that expectations remain relevant and attainable.

Reflective Questions:

- How do I manage changes in expectations?
- How can I adjust my expectations to reflect new circumstances or information?
- How do I handle situations where expectations are not met?

ANTICIPATE: PLANNING AND FORESEEING CHALLENGES

Anticipating involves planning for potential challenges and obstacles. By foreseeing possible issues, you can prepare proactive strategies to address them, minimising their impact on your goals and responsibilities.

Identifying Potential Obstacles

Think about the challenges that could arise in your current projects or responsibilities. What are the potential risks or obstacles? Identifying these factors early allows you to develop contingency plans, reducing the likelihood of being caught off guard.

Reflective Questions:

- What potential challenges or obstacles could affect my goals?
- How can I prepare for these challenges in advance?
- What contingency plans can I put in place to address potential issues?

Developing Proactive Strategies

Once you have identified potential obstacles, develop strategies to mitigate these risks. This might include acquiring additional resources, building new skills, or establishing alternative plans. Being proactive not only helps in managing risks but also builds resilience.

Reflective Questions:

- What strategies can I develop to address identified challenges?
- How can I enhance my skills or resources to better handle these challenges?
- How can I maintain a proactive mindset in my planning?

REVIEW: REFLECTING AND LEARNING

Regular review and reflection are essential for accountability. This process involves assessing your actions and outcomes, learning from your experiences, and making adjustments as needed.

Self-Reflection and Assessment

Take time to reflect on your recent actions and their outcomes. What worked well, and what didn't? Self-reflection helps you understand your strengths and areas for improvement, providing valuable insights for future actions.

Reflective Questions:

- How often do I reflect on my actions and their outcomes?
- What have I learned from my recent experiences?
- How can I apply these lessons to improve my future actions?

Continuous Improvement

Accountability is an ongoing process that requires a commitment to continuous improvement. This commitment involves regularly setting new goals, seeking feedback, and adapting your strategies to meet evolving challenges and opportunities.

Reflective Questions:

- How committed am I to continuous improvement?
- What new goals can I set to further my personal and professional growth?
- How can I maintain motivation and focus on my journey towards accountability?

By embracing the SPEAR acronym for Being Accountable—Situation, Processes, Expectations, Anticipate, and Review—you can enhance your self-awareness, build stronger relationships, and achieve greater personal and professional growth. This chapter provides a comprehensive guide to understanding and implementing accountability in your life, fostering a proactive and responsible approach to challenges and opportunities. In the next chapter, we will explore the concept of being resourceful, focusing on how to leverage your strengths and resources to overcome challenges and achieve your goals.

CHAPTER 19 - RESOURCEFUL - LEVERAGING YOUR ASSETS

BEING resourceful involves effectively using the resources available to you, including knowledge, skills, relationships, and tools. It's about being creative and adaptive in solving problems and achieving your goals. This chapter explores the elements of being resourceful through the KITS framework: Knowledge, Individuals, Tools, and Sites.

KNOWLEDGE: LEVERAGING WHAT YOU KNOW

Knowledge is a powerful resource. It encompasses the information, skills, and expertise you acquire over time. Leveraging your knowledge effectively can help you navigate challenges, make informed decisions, and innovate.

Building and Using Knowledge

Begin by assessing your current knowledge base. What do you know well, and what areas could use further development? Continuous learning is crucial for staying relevant and effective in any field. Seek out opportunities to expand your knowledge through reading, training, courses, and practical experience.

Reflective Questions:

- What are my areas of expertise, and how do I use them?
- What gaps exist in my knowledge, and how can I address them?
- How can I incorporate continuous learning into my routine?

Sharing and Applying Knowledge

Sharing your knowledge with others can reinforce your understanding and foster a collaborative environment. Additionally, applying what you know to solve real-world problems helps solidify your skills and contribute to personal and professional growth.

Reflective Questions:

- How can I share my knowledge with others in a meaningful way?
- In what ways can I apply my knowledge to current challenges?
- What opportunities exist for me to mentor or teach others?

INDIVIDUALS: BUILDING AND NURTURING RELATIONSHIPS

People are one of your most valuable resources. Building and nurturing relationships can open doors to new opportunities, provide support and guidance, and enhance your overall well-being.

Networking and Collaboration

Networking involves connecting with others in your field or areas of interest. It's about building mutually beneficial relationships that can provide insights, advice, and opportunities. Collaboration with others can lead to innovative solutions and shared success.

Reflective Questions:

- Who are the key individuals in my network, and how do I engage with them?
- How can I expand my network to include new contacts in relevant fields?
- What collaborative opportunities can I explore?

Seeking Mentorship and Support

Mentorship can provide valuable guidance and perspective. Seek out mentors who can offer insights based on their experiences and who can help you navigate your personal and professional journey. Additionally, don't hesitate to seek support from peers, friends, and family when needed.

Reflective Questions:

- Who can I turn to for mentorship and advice?
- How can I build and maintain a supportive network?
- What steps can I take to give and receive support within my community?

TOOLS: USING RESOURCES EFFECTIVELY

Tools are the tangible and intangible resources that help you achieve your goals. These can range from technology and software to personal development resources and organisational systems.

Identifying Useful Tools

Identify the tools that can enhance your productivity and effectiveness. This might include software for project management, communication platforms, or personal development resources like books and courses. It's important to choose tools that are suited to your specific needs and to learn how to use them effectively.

Reflective Questions:

- What tools do I currently use, and how effective are they?
- Are there tools that I am not using fully or effectively?
- What new tools could I explore to enhance my work and personal life?

Maximising Tool Efficiency

Using tools efficiently means understanding their features and integrating them into your workflow seamlessly. Regularly review the tools you use and ensure they continue to meet your needs. Stay open to adopting new tools that offer better solutions.

Reflective Questions:

- How can I improve my use of current tools to increase efficiency?
- What training or learning do I need to maximise the use of my tools?
- How do I evaluate new tools to ensure they meet my needs?

SITES: LEVERAGING LOCATIONS AND RESOURCES

Sites refer to both physical and digital spaces that provide resources, information, and opportunities for growth. These include libraries, educational institutions, online platforms, and community centers.

Physical Sites

Physical sites such as libraries, community centers, and educational institutions offer a wealth of resources, including books, workshops, and networking opportunities. Using these sites can enhance your knowledge and connect you with like-minded individuals.

Reflective Questions:

- What physical sites do I currently use to support my learning and growth?

- How can I explore new sites to expand my resources and opportunities?
- What local community centers or institutions can provide additional support?

Digital Sites

Digital sites include online platforms, websites, and social media networks that offer vast resources and connectivity. From online courses and webinars to forums and professional networks, these sites provide access to information and communities that can support your personal and professional development.

Reflective Questions:

- What digital sites and platforms do I currently use for learning and networking?
- How can I better use these sites to achieve my goals?
- What new digital resources can I explore to enhance my knowledge and skills?

Integrating Resourcefulness into Daily Life

Being resourceful is an ongoing process that involves continuously leveraging and optimising your knowledge, relationships, tools, and sites. By integrating these elements into your daily life, you can enhance your ability to solve problems, achieve your goals, and adapt to new challenges.

Reflective Questions:

- How resourceful do I feel in my current life and work situations?
- What areas can I improve to enhance my resourcefulness?
- How can I continue to develop my skills and resources to better handle future challenges?

By cultivating resourcefulness, you become more capable of navigating life's complexities and seizing opportunities. This chapter has explored how to leverage the KITS acronym—Knowledge, Individuals, Tools, and Sites—to enhance your resourcefulness. In the next chapter, we will go into the concept of being influential, focusing on how to positively impact others and develop meaningful connections.

CHAPTER 20 - INFLUENTIAL - CREATING POSITIVE IMPACT

HAVING COVERED the foundational RAMP factors—Resourceful, Accountable, Mind/Body State, and Purposeful—you've equipped yourself with essential tools for self-coaching and personal growth. These elements lay the groundwork for effectively managing yourself and your goals. To truly amplify your impact and effectiveness, it's essential to embrace the IT factors: Influential and True. These factors elevate your self-coaching journey, enhancing your ability to positively impact others and live authentically.

INFLUENTIAL: EXTENDING YOUR REACH

Being influential involves positively affecting others' thoughts, behaviours, and feelings. It's about being a role model, communicator, and catalyst for change, using your presence and actions to inspire and motivate others. Influence is built not on control, but on fostering a genuine connection and understanding. This chapter explores the "Influential" factor through the RIIS framework: Release, Interest, Intent, and Share.

RELEASE: LETTING GO OF CONTROL

To be influential, you must first release the desire to control others. True influence comes from inspiring and empowering people, not from dictating their actions. Letting go of control fosters an environment of trust and respect, where individuals feel free to express themselves and explore their potential.

Understanding Control vs. Influence

Recognise the difference between control and influence. Control involves directing outcomes and behaviours, often leading to resistance and resentment. Influence, however, is about guiding and inspiring through example, allowing others to make their own choices and grow independently.

Reflective Questions:

- In what areas of my life do I tend to try to control outcomes?
- How does this need for control impact my relationships and effectiveness?
- What steps can I take to shift from a mindset of control to one of influence?

Fostering Trust and Autonomy

Building influence involves creating a space where others feel trusted and autonomous. This means providing guidance and support while allowing individuals to find their path. Trust is built through consistency, honesty, and a willingness to listen and understand.

Reflective Questions:

- How do I currently build trust with those around me?
- In what ways can I encourage others' autonomy and growth?
- How can I demonstrate trust in others' abilities and decisions?

INTEREST: SHOWING GENUINE CURIOSITY

Being genuinely interested in others is a powerful way to build influence. This involves active listening, empathetic understanding, and showing that you value others' perspectives and experiences. When people feel heard and understood, they are more likely to be open to your influence.

Active Listening and Engagement

Active listening is a skill that involves fully concentrating, understanding, responding, and remembering what is being said. It goes beyond hearing words to understanding the emotions and intentions behind them. Engaging with others' ideas and feelings fosters a deeper connection and builds mutual respect.

Reflective Questions:

- How well do I practise active listening in my daily interactions?
- What can I do to show more genuine interest in others' viewpoints and experiences?
- How can I improve my ability to engage meaningfully with others?

Empathy and Understanding

Empathy involves putting yourself in others' shoes, understanding their feelings and perspectives without judgment. It is one of the biggest helping factors for building influence as it helps you connect on an emotional level and fosters a supportive and understanding environment.

Reflective Questions:

- How empathetic am I in my interactions with others?

- What can I do to better understand and relate to others' experiences?
- How does demonstrating empathy enhance my ability to influence others?

INTENT: ACTING WITH PURPOSE

Intentionality in your actions is central to being influential. This means being clear about your goals, values, and the message you want to convey. People are drawn to those who act with clarity and purpose, as it signals confidence and direction.

Clarity of Purpose

Being clear about your intentions helps others understand your motivations and aligns them with your vision. This clarity not only guides your actions but also provides a consistent message that others can trust and follow.

Reflective Questions:

- What are my core values and intentions, and how do they shape my actions?
- How can I communicate my intentions more clearly and authentically?
- How do my actions reflect my commitment to positive change?

Consistency and Authenticity

Consistency in your actions and authenticity in your behaviour build credibility and influence. When people see that your actions align with your stated values and beliefs, they are more likely to trust and be influenced by you.

Reflective Questions:

- Are my actions consistently aligned with my stated values?
- How transparent am I in my interactions and decisions?
- What steps can I take to increase my consistency and authenticity?

SHARE: COMMUNICATING AND SHARING KNOWLEDGE

Sharing knowledge and experiences is a cornerstone of influence. Whether through mentoring, teaching, or simply engaging in conversations, sharing helps to disseminate valuable ideas and encourages others to grow and learn. It also demonstrates generosity and a commitment to the collective good.

Mentoring and Teaching

Mentoring involves guiding others based on your own experiences and insights. It's an opportunity to share wisdom, offer guidance, and help others navigate their challenges. Teaching, on the other hand, focuses on imparting specific skills or knowledge, helping others build their capabilities.

Reflective Questions:

- What knowledge or experiences can I share that might benefit others?
- How can I find opportunities to teach, mentor, or share my insights?
- How do I ensure that my sharing is supportive and empowering rather than overwhelming or prescriptive?

Engaging and Empowering

Effective sharing is not just about imparting information but also about engaging and empowering others. This means creating opportunities for dialogue, encouraging others to share their ideas, and fostering a collaborative environment where everyone can contribute.

Reflective Questions:

- How can I create opportunities for others to share their ideas and experiences?
- What can I do to empower others to take initiative and lead?
- How does my approach to sharing influence the way others perceive and interact with me?

INTEGRATING THE INFLUENTIAL FACTOR

Integrating the "Influential" factor into your self-coaching practise involves a combination of releasing control, showing genuine interest, acting with intent, and sharing your knowledge. These elements work together to create a powerful influence that inspires and uplifts those around you.

Reflective Questions:

- How can I balance influencing others with respecting their autonomy?
- What steps can I take to enhance my influential presence in various aspects of my life?
- How can I measure the impact of my influence on others and continually improve?

By embracing the "Influential" factor, you enhance not only your personal growth but also your ability to positively impact others. This chapter has explored how to extend your reach and create a meaningful impact through the RIIS acronym—Release, Interest, Intent, and Share. Next, we will explore the "True" factor, focusing on the importance of authenticity in your self-coaching journey and in building deeper, more meaningful connections.

CHAPTER 21 - TRUE - EMBRACING AUTHENTICITY

AFTER DEVELOPING the foundational RAMP factors and exploring the influential aspects, the final step in enhancing your self-coaching practise is embracing authenticity through the "True" factor. This factor emphasises living in alignment with your true self, fostering genuine connections, and cultivating integrity in all aspects of life. The "True" factor is examined through the VAST acronym: Vulnerable, Authentic, Sincere, and Transparent.

TRUE: EMBRACING AUTHENTICITY

Authenticity involves being true to yourself and expressing your genuine thoughts, feelings, and values. It means living in a way that is congruent with who you are, rather than conforming to external expectations or pressures. Authenticity builds trust and respect, both with yourself and with others, and it leads to deeper, more meaningful relationships.

VULNERABLE: THE COURAGE TO BE SEEN

Vulnerability is often misunderstood as a weakness, but it is actually a profound strength. Being vulnerable means allowing yourself to be seen as you truly are, with all your flaws, fears, and insecurities. It involves taking risks in relationships and being open to emotional exposure.

Embracing Vulnerability

To embrace vulnerability, you must first accept yourself completely, including your imperfections. This acceptance allows you to engage with others more openly and authentically, creating a space where true connections can flourish.

Reflective Questions:

- What fears or insecurities do I have about being vulnerable?
- How can I embrace these aspects of myself without shame?
- In what ways can vulnerability enhance my relationships and personal growth?

Cultivating Courage

Vulnerability requires courage—the courage to show up, speak your truth, and face the possibility of rejection or misunderstanding. This courage is not about the absence of fear, but about moving forward despite it, knowing that authenticity is more valuable than perfection.

Reflective Questions:

- How can I cultivate the courage to be vulnerable in my interactions?
- What small steps can I take to practise vulnerability in safe environments?
- How does being vulnerable impact my self-confidence and authenticity?

AUTHENTIC: LIVING IN ALIGNMENT WITH YOUR VALUES

Authenticity is about aligning your actions, words, and choices with your core values and beliefs. It means being honest about who you are and what you stand for, and living in a way that reflects these truths.

Identifying Core Values

Start by identifying your core values—the principles that guide your decisions and actions. These values are the foundation of your authenticity, helping you navigate life's challenges with integrity and clarity.

Reflective Questions:

- What are my core values, and how do they influence my decisions?
- Are there areas in my life where I feel disconnected from my values?
- How can I bring my actions more in line with my core beliefs?

EXPRESSING AUTHENTICITY

Expressing AUTHENTICITY involves being truthful in your interactions, showing up as your true self, and refusing to hide behind facades or social masks. It means honouring your own needs and boundaries while respecting those of others.

Reflective Questions:

- How do I currently express my authenticity in my relationships and work?
- What fears or obstacles prevent me from being fully authentic?
- How can I create more opportunities to express my true self?

SINCERE: GENUINE COMMUNICATION AND ACTIONS

Sincerity involves being genuine and honest in your communication and actions. It means saying what you mean and meaning what you say, without hidden agendas or manipulation. Sincerity builds trust and fosters open, honest relationships.

Genuine Communication

To communicate sincerely, focus on being clear and honest in your interactions. Avoid manipulation or saying what you think others want to hear. Instead, share your thoughts and feelings openly, and listen to others with respect and empathy.

Reflective Questions:

- How can I improve my communication to be more sincere and honest?
- What situations make it difficult for me to be genuine, and why?
- How can I ensure that my words and actions consistently reflect my true intentions?

Consistent Actions

Sincerity also involves consistency between your words and actions. When you commit to something, follow through. This consistency not only builds trust but also reinforces your integrity and reliability.

Reflective Questions:

- Are my actions consistent with my promises and commitments?
- How can I better align my actions with my words to maintain sincerity?
- What can I do to build a reputation for honesty and reliability?

TRANSPARENT: OPENNESS AND HONESTY

Transparency is about being open and honest in your dealings with others. It involves sharing information, being clear about your intentions, and being willing to expose your true self, even when it feels uncomfortable. Transparency fosters trust and encourages others to be open and honest in return.

Openness in Communication

Transparency in communication means being clear and straightforward, without withholding information or hiding behind ambiguity. This openness helps to build trust and prevents misunderstandings.

Reflective Questions:

- How transparent am I in my communication with others?
- What fears or concerns prevent me from being fully open?
- How can I cultivate a habit of transparency in my daily interactions?

Honesty in Intentions

Being transparent also involves being honest about your intentions and motivations. This honesty helps others understand where you are coming from and fosters a culture of openness and mutual respect.

Reflective Questions:

- How clear am I about my intentions and motivations when interacting with others?
- In what situations do I tend to withhold information, and why?
- How can I practise greater honesty in expressing my intentions and goals?

INTEGRATING THE TRUE FACTOR

Integrating the "True" factor into your life involves embracing vulnerability, living authentically, communicating sincerely, and practising transparency. These elements help you build deeper, more meaningful relationships and create a life that is aligned with your true self.

Reflective Questions:

- How can I practise vulnerability and authenticity more consistently in my life?
- What steps can I take to improve sincerity and transparency in my interactions?
- How does living true to myself impact my relationships and overall well-being?

By embracing the "True" factor, you not only enhance your personal authenticity but also contribute to a more honest and open environment for those around you. This chapter has explored how to live in alignment with your true self through the VAST framework—Vulnerable, Authentic, Sincere, and Transparent. As you integrate these principles into your self-coaching practise, you will find greater fulfillment, deeper connections, and a more profound sense of purpose in your journey.

PART FIVE

PART V - APPLICATION AND WHAT'S NEXT

CHAPTER 22 - RELATING THE FOUR ELEMENTS TO EVERYDAY SITUATIONS

INTEGRATING BE ELEMENTS AND RAMP-IT FACTORS FOR EFFECTIVE SELF-COACHING

THE BE elements and RAMP-IT factors work together to create a comprehensive framework for self-coaching, helping you remain present, calm, and effective in any situation. Whether you are starting a new journey, feeling stuck, or scaling up to new heights, understanding and integrating these elements and factors can enhance your ability to navigate challenges and achieve personal growth.

RECAP: BE ELEMENTS- THE FOUNDATION OF EMOTIONAL WELL-BEING

The BE elements—Safety, Gain and Loss, Clarity and Confusion, and Self and Ego—represent fundamental aspects of human psychology and emotional well-being. They explain the root causes of our emotions, triggers, and behaviours, providing a foundation for understanding why we react the way we do in different situations.

Safety: Feeling secure in your environment mentally, emotionally, and physically. A sense of safety allows you to be calm and open to new experiences.

Gain and Loss: Perceptions of gain or loss in various aspects of life. Understanding this element helps you manage emotional responses to life's ups and downs.

Clarity and Confusion: Having a clear understanding of situations and goals. Clarity reduces anxiety and enhances decision-making.

Self and Ego: Distinguishing between a healthy sense of self-worth and an inflated ego. A balanced self fosters positive relationships and personal growth.

RECAP: RAMP-IT FACTORS- THE PILLARS OF SELF-COACHING

The RAMP-IT framework consists of six main factors, each with specific sub-factors that guide personal development and self-improvement. Together, these factors form the pillars of effective self-coaching.

Purposeful: Acting with intention and understanding the broader purpose behind your actions. It includes Role, Intent, Cause, and Service.

Mind/Body State: Integrating mental and physical well-being through supportive environments, acceptance, recognising physical feelings, managing thoughts, and regulating emotions.

Accountable: Taking responsibility for your actions and decisions by understanding the situation, establishing processes, setting expectations, anticipating challenges, and reviewing progress.

Resourceful: Effectively using available resources such as knowledge, individuals, tools, and sites to achieve your goals.

Influential: You can positively impact others by leading by example, communicating effectively, showing genuine interest, and sharing experiences.

True: Living authentically, sincerely, and transparently by embracing vulnerability, staying true to your values, and maintaining transparency.

WORKING TOGETHER: BE ELEMENTS AND RAMP-IT FACTORS

When integrated, the BE elements and RAMP-IT factors provide a holistic approach to self-coaching, enabling you to be present and calm in any situation, whether you're starting something new, stuck and wanting to level up, or scaling up to new heights of accomplishment.

Starting:

At the beginning of a journey, clarity (BE) combined with purposeful intent (RAMP-IT) helps you define your goals and set a clear path forward. Ensuring safety (BE) and creating supportive routines (RAMP-IT) provide a stable foundation for growth.

Stuck:

When feeling stuck, understanding your current situation (Accountable) and recognising emotional triggers (Gain and Loss) can help you identify barriers. Leveraging knowledge (Resourceful) and seeking clarity (Clarity and Confusion) allow you to find new perspectives and solutions.

Scaling Up:

As you scale up to new heights, balancing self and ego (BE) with true authenticity (RAMP-IT) ensures you remain grounded. Effective communication (Influential) and maintaining mental and physical well-being (Mind/Body State) support sustainable growth.

PRACTICAL INTEGRATION: DAILY PRACTISES

Daily Check-Ins: Regularly assess your BE elements and RAMP-IT factors. Reflect on your emotional state, goals, and progress.

Mindfulness and Meditation: practise mindfulness to stay present and aware of your thoughts, emotions, and physical sensations.

Goal Setting and Review: Set SMART goals that align with your purpose and regularly review your progress. Adjust your actions based on feedback and self-reflection.

Supportive Routines: Establish routines that promote emotional regulation and personal growth. Incorporate self-care, learning, and meaningful connections into your daily life.

Don't forget to use the shortcut from earlier in the book!

The integration of BE elements and RAMP-IT factors offers a powerful framework for self-coaching, enabling you to remain present, calm, and effective in any situation. By understanding and applying these concepts, you can navigate challenges with resilience, achieve personal growth, and live a more balanced and fulfilling life.

POINTS TO PONDER:

- How do the BE elements and RAMP-IT factors interact in your daily life?
- What practises can you implement to integrate these elements and factors more effectively?
- How can this integrated approach enhance your ability to be present and calm in various situations?

Self-Reflection Questions:

- How do the BE elements influence your emotional responses and behaviours?
- In what ways do the RAMP-IT factors guide your actions and decisions?
- How can you leverage the synergy between BE elements and RAMP-IT factors to achieve your goals?

- What specific daily practises can help you integrate these concepts into your life?

CHAPTER 23 - APPLYING THE BE ELEMENTS FOR COMMON SITUATIONS

THESE SHORT OVERVIEWS are just that: a simple, brief look at how we can be affected by the BE Elements in facing obstacles and how understanding how to use the BE Elements and RAMPIT Framework together can find solutions to overcome them.

While these short examples are just a summary, I decided to expand on these as I was publishing this book and have created a PDF with all of these in more detail, breaking down the BE Elements and RAMPIT Factors.

You can access it here:

https://nolancollins.com/be-applied

THE OVERVIEWS ARE AS FOLLOWS:

- Building Confidence
- Overcoming Procrastination
- Setting Goals
- Conflict Resolution

- Parenting (short short version!!)
- Meetings
- Dealing with Toxic and Narcissistic Behaviour
- Overcoming Imposter Syndrome
- Being Controlling - How to Stop
- Dealing with Grief
- Feeling the Need to Validate Yourself
- How to Stop People Pleasing
- Overcoming Nice Guy - or Gal, Behaviour
- Dealing with Attachment Styles

BUILDING CONFIDENCE

Building confidence involves overcoming self-doubt, fear of failure, and hesitancy in taking risks. This is essential for personal and professional growth.

The BE elements—Safety, Gain and Loss, Clarity, and Self vs. Ego—provide a foundation for addressing the emotional and psychological barriers to confidence. Creating a sense of internal safety allows individuals to take risks without fear of judgment while understanding the balance of gain and loss helps manage expectations and motivates action. Clarity in goals and self-perception reduces uncertainty, and differentiating between self and ego ensures that confidence is rooted in authentic values rather than external validation.

The RAMPIT framework further supports confidence-building through structured strategies. **Purposeful** actions involve understanding one's roles, setting clear intentions, connecting goals to a larger cause, and engaging in meaningful service. **Mind/Body State** emphasises creating a supportive environment, accepting current progress, and managing physical feelings, thoughts, and emotions. **Accountable** involves setting realistic goals, anticipating challenges, and regularly reviewing progress. **Resourceful** encourages leveraging knowledge, networks, tools, and sites to support growth. **Influential** highlights the importance of inspiring others through authenticity and sharing knowledge, while **True** emphasises living in alignment with one's core values, embracing vulnerability, and being transparent and sincere.

By integrating the BE elements and the RAMPIT framework, individuals can cultivate sustainable and resilient confidence. This holistic approach addresses both internal and external factors, ensuring that confidence is built on a solid foundation and is adaptable to challenges.

OVERCOMING PROCRASTINATION

Procrastination is a common barrier to productivity, characterised by delaying tasks or decisions, often leading to stress and missed opportunities. Addressing procrastination involves understanding the underlying emotional and psychological factors that contribute to this behaviour.

The BE elements—Clarity, Safety, Gain and Loss, and Self vs. Ego—play a large role in overcoming procrastination. Clarity helps in defining tasks and goals, reducing ambiguity and making it easier to take action. Establishing a sense of safety allows individuals to address fears and anxieties without fear of judgment, while understanding the balance of gain and loss emphasises the benefits of taking action. Differentiating between tasks aligned with one's true self and those driven by external pressures helps prioritise efforts effectively.

The RAMPIT framework provides practical strategies to tackle procrastination. **Purposeful** actions focus on clarifying roles, setting intentions, connecting tasks to a larger cause, and viewing tasks as a form of service. **Mind/Body State** involves creating an optimal environment, accepting current progress, and managing feelings, thoughts, and emotions that contribute to procrastination. **Accountable** emphasises the importance of setting clear goals, establishing processes, anticipating challenges, and regularly reviewing progress. **Resourceful** encourages using available resources, including knowledge, skills, relationships, and tools, to support productivity. **Influential** focuses on inspiring oneself and others to take action, while **True** involves living authentically, embracing vulnerability, and being transparent about challenges.

Combining the BE elements and the RAMPIT framework provides a comprehensive approach to overcoming procrastination. This approach helps individuals address both the root causes of procrastination and the practical steps needed to increase productivity and achieve their goals.

SETTING GOALS

Setting goals is a much-needed and often overlooked aspect of personal and professional growth. Many people struggle with it due to uncertainty, lack of clarity, fear of failure, or feeling overwhelmed. Effective goal-setting helps provide direction, motivation, and efficient use of time and resources.

The BE elements—Clarity, Safety, Gain and Loss, and Self vs. Ego—play a significant role in overcoming these challenges. Clarity involves defining specific outcomes and understanding the reasons behind them, which helps focus efforts and reduce indecision. Establishing a sense of safety allows individuals to set ambitious goals without fear of judgment while acknowledging the potential gains and losses of achieving these goals helps maintain motivation and realistic expectations. Differentiating between authentic desires and ego-driven motivations ensures that goals are meaningful and aligned with one's true values.

The RAMPIT framework complements this approach by offering structured strategies for setting and achieving goals. **Purposeful** actions include recognising roles, setting clear intentions, connecting goals to a broader cause, and viewing goals as a service to oneself or others. **Mind/Body State** emphasises creating a supportive environment, accepting current capabilities, and managing physical feelings, thoughts, and emotions to maintain focus and motivation. **Accountable** involves setting realistic expectations, anticipating challenges, and regularly reviewing progress to stay on track. **Resourceful** encourages using available resources, including knowledge, skills, support networks, and tools, to support goal achievement. **Influential** focuses on inspiring oneself and others, leading by example, and fostering a culture of continuous improvement, while **True** emphasises authenticity, sincerity, and transparency in the goal-setting process.

By integrating the BE elements and the RAMPIT framework, individuals can set and achieve goals that are not only ambitious and meaningful but also realistic and attainable. This holistic approach helps ensure that goals are aligned with personal values and are pursued with commitment and resilience, leading to sustained growth and fulfilment.

CONFLICT RESOLUTION

Conflict resolution is essential for maintaining healthy relationships, fostering collaboration, and creating a positive environment. Challenges in resolving conflicts can arise from poor communication, emotional reactivity, power dynamics, or misunderstandings, leading to strained relationships, reduced collaboration, and increased stress.

Understanding the BE elements—Clarity, Safety, Gain and Loss, and Self vs. Ego—aids in navigating conflicts. Clarity involves understanding the root causes of conflicts and communicating needs and boundaries effectively. Safety creates an environment where all parties feel respected and heard, facilitating honest and open dialogue. Recognising the potential gains from resolving conflicts and the losses from avoiding them helps motivate constructive engagement. Differentiating between genuine needs and ego-driven desires ensures that resolutions are meaningful and focused on mutual benefit.

The RAMPIT framework further supports conflict resolution through structured strategies. **Purposeful** actions involve understanding roles, setting clear intentions, connecting the resolution to a larger cause, and engaging in actions that foster mutual respect and understanding. **Mind/Body State** emphasises creating an optimal environment, accepting emotions and perspectives, and managing physical sensations, thoughts, and emotions that arise during conflicts. **Accountable** involves taking responsibility, establishing clear processes, setting realistic expectations, and regularly reviewing progress as a solution-focused way forward. **Resourceful** encourages leveraging support networks, mediation tools, and communication technologies. **Influential** focuses on leading by example, encouraging open communication, and fostering a culture of respect and cooperation, while **True** emphasises authenticity, vulnerability, sincerity, and transparency in interactions, essentially being honest about your intentions, ego, and need to be in control or really find a solution.

By integrating the BE elements and the RAMPIT framework, individuals can approach conflict resolution with empathy, structure, and a focus on positive outcomes. This comprehensive approach addresses both the emotional and practical aspects of conflicts, promoting healthier relationships and more effective problem-solving.

PARENTING

(you can also read my book **RAMP your Parenting** for more depth on this topic- available on my website and Amazon)

Effective parenting involves nurturing, guiding, and supporting children's development while balancing discipline with empathy. Challenges in parenting, such as communication barriers, emotional stress, and inconsistent discipline, can impact the parent-child relationship and overall family dynamics.

The BE elements—Safety, Gain and Loss, Clarity, and Self vs. Ego—are fundamental in navigating these challenges. Creating a safe environment, both physically and emotionally, is crucial for fostering open communication and trust. Understanding the gains of positive parenting and the losses from negative behaviours motivates consistent and constructive approaches. Clarity in communication and expectations helps establish consistent rules and boundaries, while distinguishing between the child's needs and parental ego ensures a nurturing environment focused on the child's well-being.

The RAMPIT framework offers structured strategies to enhance parenting effectiveness. **Purposeful** parenting involves understanding parental roles, setting clear intentions, connecting daily practises to broader goals, and viewing parenting as a service to the child's growth. **Mind/Body State** emphasises creating a supportive home environment, accepting the challenges of parenting, and managing physical sensations, thoughts, and emotions to maintain a balanced and patient approach. **Accountable** parenting includes demonstrating responsibility, establishing consistent practises, setting realistic expectations, and regularly reviewing and adapting strategies. **Resourceful** involves leveraging support networks, educational resources, and tools to enhance parenting skills and knowledge. **Influential** parenting focuses on leading by example, fostering a culture of respect and empathy, and encouraging open communication, while **True** emphasises authenticity, sincerity, and transparency in interactions with children.

By integrating the BE elements and the RAMPIT framework, parents can address both the emotional and practical aspects of parenting. This holistic approach helps in creating a positive, nurturing environment that promotes the healthy development of children and strengthens family relationships.

MEETINGS

This may seem like a strange topic to include in this book, however I found most of us have to attend meetings a lot these days, and it was because of some uncomfortable ones, for me and other attendees that much of what I’ve developed was created.

Effective meetings are essential for organizational communication and decision-making but often face challenges such as lack of focus, poor time management, unclear objectives, and ineffective communication. These issues can lead to wasted time, frustration, and unproductive outcomes.

The BE elements—Clarity, Safety, Gain and Loss, and Self vs. Ego—are fundamental in addressing these challenges. Clarity ensures that objectives and agendas are well-defined, helping participants understand the meeting's purpose and expected outcomes. Creating a safe environment fosters open communication and active participation, while recognising the potential gains from a well-conducted meeting motivates better planning and execution. Balancing contributions with humility helps maintain a collaborative atmosphere, avoiding ego-driven disruptions.

The RAMPIT framework provides structured strategies to enhance meeting effectiveness. **Purposeful** meetings involve setting clear objectives, defining participant roles, and aligning the agenda with broader organisational goals. **Mind/Body State** emphasises creating a conducive environment, accepting diverse opinions, and managing physical sensations, thoughts, and emotions to maintain focus and a positive atmosphere. **Accountable** practises include setting clear expectations, establishing processes for decision-making and follow-up, and regularly reviewing meeting effectiveness. **Resourceful** strategies involve leveraging tools and technologies for planning and documentation, using networks for support, and accessing resources for best practises. **Influential** focuses on leading by example, encouraging equal participation, and fostering a culture of respect and collaboration, while **True** emphasises authenticity, sincerity, and transparency in interactions.

By integrating the BE elements and the RAMPIT framework, organisations can transform meetings into productive, inclusive, and effective events. This comprehensive approach addresses both the emotional and practical aspects of meetings, enhancing collaboration, decision-making, and overall productivity.

DEALING WITH TOXIC AND NARCISSISTIC BEHAVIOUR

Dealing with toxic and narcissistic behaviour in personal and professional relationships is challenging due to manipulation, lack of empathy, and excessive self-centeredness. These behaviours can cause emotional distress, damage relationships, and reduce productivity.

The BE elements—Safety, Gain and Loss, Clarity, and Self vs. Ego—are essential in managing these situations. Establishing emotional safety involves setting boundaries and seeking support, which is critical for protecting oneself. Understanding the gains of distancing from toxicity versus the losses of staying in harmful environments helps in making informed decisions. Clarity aids in recognising harmful behaviours and communicating boundaries effectively, while balancing self-respect with humility prevents ego-driven conflicts.

The RAMPIT framework offers practical strategies for addressing toxic and narcissistic behaviour. **Purposeful** actions involve setting intentional boundaries, understanding roles in relationships, and focusing on personal well-being and growth. **Mind/Body State** emphasises creating supportive environments, accepting what cannot be changed, and managing stress and emotional responses. **Accountable** practises include taking responsibility for one's responses, setting and enforcing boundaries, and seeking support when necessary. **Resourceful** strategies involve using counselling, support networks, and tools to manage interactions and protect well-being. **Influential** focuses on leading by example, maintaining integrity, and fostering a culture of respect and accountability, while **True** emphasises authenticity, sincerity, and transparency in interactions.

By integrating the BE elements and the RAMPIT framework, individuals can effectively navigate toxic and narcissistic behaviours, fostering healthier relationships and environments. This comprehensive approach addresses both the emotional and practical aspects of dealing with such behaviours, ensuring personal safety and well-being while promoting positive outcomes.

OVERCOMING IMPOSTER SYNDROME

Imposter syndrome is a psychological pattern characterised by persistent self-doubt and fear of being exposed as a "fraud," despite evident competence. This syndrome can hinder personal and professional growth by causing anxiety, stress, and avoidance of new opportunities.

The BE elements—Safety, Gain and Loss, Clarity, and Self vs. Ego—are help in addressing these issues. Establishing a safe mental space allows individuals to acknowledge imposter feelings without judgment. Understanding the benefits of embracing achievements and recognising the value of one's contributions can help build confidence. Clarity in identifying triggers and reframing negative beliefs, along with differentiating genuine self-assessment from ego-driven perfectionism, supports a more realistic self-view.

The RAMPIT framework provides structured strategies to combat imposter syndrome. **Purposeful** actions include setting clear goals, understanding one's roles, and connecting achievements to broader missions, which reinforces a sense of purpose and validation. **Mind/Body State** emphasises creating supportive environments, accepting imposter feelings as common, and managing stress and emotional responses to maintain balance. **Accountable** practises involve taking ownership of achievements, setting realistic goals, and regularly reviewing progress to foster a positive self-assessment. **Resourceful** strategies encourage leveraging support networks, professional development, and tools for tracking progress and celebrating achievements. **Influential** focuses on sharing experiences, encouraging others, and fostering a culture of confidence and self-acceptance, while **True** emphasises authenticity, sincerity, and transparency in interactions.

By integrating the BE elements and the RAMPIT framework, individuals can effectively overcome imposter syndrome, fostering greater confidence, self-acceptance, and a more positive outlook on their abilities and achievements. This holistic approach not only addresses the emotional challenges associated with imposter syndrome but also provides practical steps for continuous growth and self-improvement.

BEING CONTROLLING: HOW TO STOP

Controlling behaviour often stems from a need for certainty and fear of uncertainty, manifesting in micromanagement or strict control over others' actions. This behaviour can strain relationships, increase stress, and stifle creativity.

Understanding the BE elements—Safety, Gain and Loss, Clarity, and Self vs. Ego—aids in understanding and modifying controlling tendencies. Establishing a sense of internal safety can reduce the anxiety that drives the need to control. Recognising the benefits of relinquishing control, such as improved trust and relationships, versus the drawbacks of maintaining it, helps shift behaviour. Clarity in understanding the motivations behind controlling actions and differentiating genuine concern from ego-driven desires supports more balanced interactions.

The RAMPIT framework provides a structured approach to reduce controlling behaviour. **Purposeful** actions involve redefining roles to emphasise support over control, setting intentions for trust and respect, and aligning these behaviours with broader goals of fostering healthy relationships. **Mind/Body State** focuses on creating environments that support openness, accepting uncertainty, and managing stress and emotions associated with the need to control. **Accountable** practises include acknowledging the impact of controlling behaviour, setting realistic expectations for change, and regularly reviewing progress. **Resourceful** strategies involve leveraging support networks, counselling, and self-help resources to aid in behaviour modification. **Influential** emphasises leading by example, encouraging autonomy, and fostering a culture of mutual respect, while **True** highlights the importance of authenticity, sincerity, and transparency in interactions.

By integrating the BE elements and the RAMPIT framework, individuals can effectively reduce controlling behaviours, fostering healthier and more supportive relationships. This comprehensive approach addresses both the emotional and practical aspects of managing controlling tendencies, promoting personal growth and well-being.

DEALING WITH GRIEF

Grief is a natural response to loss, encompassing a range of emotions including sadness, anger, and confusion. It can result from various forms of loss, such as the death of a loved one, the end of a relationship, or significant life changes. Grief can lead to emotional distress, isolation, and impaired functioning.

The BE elements—Safety, Gain and Loss, Clarity, and Self vs. Ego—offer a supportive framework for navigating grief. Creating a safe emotional environment allows individuals to process grief without judgement, while acknowledging the loss helps in accepting and understanding the emotional impact. Clarity involves recognising the stages of grief and differentiating between genuine mourning and guilt or regret, which supports a focused healing process.

The RAMPIT framework provides structured approaches to manage grief. **Purposeful** actions include setting intentions for self-care and finding meaning in the grieving process, such as honouring memories or connecting grief to broader life goals. **Mind/Body State** emphasises creating supportive environments, accepting grief as a natural process, and managing physical and emotional responses. **Accountable** practises involve recognising personal responsibility in healing, setting realistic expectations, and seeking support. **Resourceful** strategies encourage using support networks, therapy, and self-help resources to navigate the complexities of grief. **Influential** focuses on sharing experiences and fostering a culture of openness and empathy, while **True** emphasises authenticity, sincerity, and transparency in expressing grief.

Integrating the BE elements and the RAMPIT framework helps individuals approach grief with compassion, structure, and a focus on healing. This holistic method addresses the emotional and practical challenges of grief, promoting personal growth, resilience, and well-being.

FEELING THE NEED TO VALIDATE YOURSELF

The need for self-validation is crucial for personal growth and well-being, yet many individuals struggle with over-reliance on external validation. This dependency can lead to insecurity, anxiety, and a lack of self-trust, stifling personal and professional growth.

The BE elements—Safety, Gain and Loss, Clarity, and Self vs. Ego—offer a framework for fostering self-validation. Establishing a sense of internal safety involves affirming one's worth and experiences without seeking external approval. Recognising the benefits of self-validation, such as increased confidence and autonomy, versus the drawbacks of seeking external validation, motivates a shift towards self-reliance. Clarity in understanding the sources of the need for validation and distinguishing constructive feedback from dependency helps in developing self-trust. Focusing on genuine self-acceptance rather than ego-driven desires for recognition is essential for true self-validation.

The RAMPIT framework provides structured strategies for building self-validation. **Purposeful** actions include setting intentions to trust oneself, understanding one's roles and values, and aligning personal achievements with internal standards. **Mind/Body State** emphasises creating environments that support positive self-reflection, accepting the need for validation as a common human experience, and managing associated emotions. **Accountable** practises involve recognising personal responsibility in building self-worth, setting realistic expectations, and seeking support when necessary. **Resourceful** strategies encourage leveraging support networks, self-help resources, and tools for tracking progress and managing emotions. **Influential** focuses on leading by example, encouraging others to trust themselves, and fostering a culture of self-reliance and confidence, while **True** highlights the importance of authenticity, sincerity, and transparency in interactions.

By integrating the BE elements and the RAMPIT framework, individuals can effectively cultivate self-validation, fostering greater self-reliance, confidence, and overall well-being. This holistic approach addresses both the emotional and practical challenges of the need for external validation, promoting personal growth and self-acceptance.

HOW TO STOP PEOPLE PLEASING

People pleasing is a common behaviour rooted in a desire for approval and fear of rejection, often leading individuals to prioritise others' needs over their own. While it can foster short-term harmony, chronic people pleasing can result in burnout, resentment, and a loss of self-identity.

The BE elements—Safety, Gain and Loss, Clarity, and Self vs. Ego—provide a framework for addressing this behaviour. Creating a safe internal environment enables individuals to assert their needs and boundaries without fear of conflict. Understanding the benefits of setting boundaries, such as increased self-respect and authentic relationships, versus the drawbacks of constant people pleasing, helps motivate change. Clarity in identifying triggers and underlying fears or beliefs that drive people pleasing behaviour aids in shifting towards more authentic interactions.

The RAMPIT framework offers structured strategies to stop people pleasing. **Purposeful** actions include understanding personal roles and values, setting clear boundaries, and aligning actions with authentic self-expression. **Mind/Body State** focuses on maintaining balance, accepting that it is impossible to please everyone, and managing the anxiety and guilt associated with boundary-setting. **Accountable** practises involve taking responsibility for one's well-being, setting realistic expectations, and seeking support when needed. **Resourceful** strategies encourage using supportive networks, self-help resources, and tools for building assertiveness. **Influential** focuses on leading by example, fostering a culture of respect and authenticity, while **True** emphasises the importance of being genuine, honest, and transparent about one's experiences.

By integrating the BE elements and the RAMPIT framework, individuals can effectively reduce people-pleasing behaviours, fostering greater self-reliance, confidence, and well-being. This comprehensive approach addresses both the emotional and practical challenges of people pleasing, promoting personal growth and self-acceptance.

OVERCOMING "NICE GUY" (OR NICE GAL) BEHAVIOUR

"Nice Guy" (or "Nice Gal") behaviour involves prioritising others' needs and desires excessively, often to gain approval or avoid conflict, at the expense of one's own well-being and authenticity. This pattern can lead to suppressed needs, inauthentic relationships, and eventually, resentment and burnout.

The BE elements—Safety, Gain and Loss, Clarity, and Self vs. Ego—offer a framework to address this behaviour by promoting self-awareness, boundary-setting, and authenticity. Establish a safe internal environment for expressing true thoughts and feelings. Understanding the benefits of authenticity, such as healthier relationships and increased self-respect, versus the drawbacks of constant agreeableness helps motivate change. Clarity involves recognising the patterns and triggers of this behaviour and differentiating between genuine kindness and the need for external validation.

The RAMPIT framework provides structured strategies to overcome "Nice Guy" or "Nice Gal" behaviour. **Purposeful** actions include understanding personal roles in relationships, setting clear boundaries, and aligning behaviour with self-respect. **Mind/Body State** focuses on maintaining emotional and physical balance, accepting that it is not possible to please everyone, and managing associated anxiety and guilt. **Accountable** practises involve recognising personal responsibility for expressing authentic needs, maintaining boundaries, and seeking support when needed. **Resourceful** strategies encourage leveraging supportive networks, self-help resources, and tools for building assertiveness. **Influential** focuses on leading by example, fostering a culture of authenticity and respect, while **True** highlights the importance of being genuine, honest, and transparent about your experiences.

By integrating the BE elements and the RAMPIT framework, individuals can effectively overcome "Nice Guy" or "Nice Gal" behaviours, fostering greater self-reliance, confidence, and authenticity. This comprehensive approach addresses both the emotional and practical challenges associated with these behaviours, promoting personal growth and genuine self-expression.

DEALING WITH ATTACHMENT STYLES

Attachment styles, such as secure, anxious, avoidant, and disorganised, describe patterns of behaviour in relationships influenced by early caregiving experiences. While secure attachment fosters healthy, balanced relationships, anxious attachment often leads to excessive need for reassurance and fear of abandonment, and avoidant attachment results in emotional distancing to protect oneself from vulnerability. These behaviours can cause emotional distress, communication barriers, and strain in relationships.

Understanding and addressing these patterns through the BE elements —Safety, Gain and Loss, Clarity, and Self vs. Ego—provides a foundation for healthier interactions. The BE elements help individuals create internal safety, recognise the benefits of secure attachment, clarify personal needs, and differentiate between genuine needs and ego-driven fears.

The RAMPIT framework offers structured strategies to manage attachment styles. **Purposeful** actions include setting clear intentions for secure and authentic relationships, understanding personal roles, and aligning behaviours with these goals. **Mind/Body State** emphasises maintaining emotional and physical balance, accepting that attachment behaviours often stem from past experiences, and managing associated feelings. **Accountable** practises involve recognising personal responsibility, setting realistic expectations, and seeking support to address attachment behaviours. **Resourceful** strategies leverage supportive networks, self-help resources, and tools for building self-confidence and managing communication. **Influential** focuses on leading by example, encouraging secure attachment, and fostering a culture of authenticity, while **True** emphasises being genuine, honest, and transparent in interactions.

By integrating the BE elements and the RAMPIT framework, individuals can address attachment concerns, whether in themselves or in their partners, fostering more secure, fulfilling relationships. This holistic approach promotes personal growth, enhances emotional intelligence, and encourages authentic self-expression, helping individuals move towards healthier relational patterns.

I HAVE TRIED to give some practical examples of using the BE Elements and RAMPIT Framework from throughout the book, although this book is primarily about you and understanding yourself, no matter the situation. In this section, I have added several specific situations that we often face to show how to apply these frameworks contextually.

Thankfully, or should I say, hopefully, we do not face all of these situations every day. I use the phrase "situational" frequently because, just as you will never have the same water run over your foot when dipping your foot in a stream at the same spot, so too will the situational factors change from one day, hour, a minute or even second to the next.

For more depth on these and other topics, please take a look at my RAMPIT RUNDOWN books, which are shorter than this book, and focus on one topic and the obstacles we face in that area. For example, Parenting, Relationships, Teenage Life (written with my teenage daughter) and I even have one for Service Staff as I spent many, many years in the hospitality industry and recognised how important self-awareness is in that industry.

CONCLUSION - THE TRANSFORMATIVE JOURNEY OF BE-ING

THE JOURNEY of BE-ing and self-coaching is a profound exploration of self-awareness, emotional regulation, and purposeful living. Throughout this book, we've explored:

The triangle of Be-ing, and learned how we can be affect ourselves when alone, by other people and we can affect others in the way we act, emote and respond.

Is it helpful? A question to ask yourself to ensure you are striving for a win-win scenario, with no ego, but looking to achieve the state of being at one with yourself, by yourself and when faced with difficult or challenging situations.

The Experience Loop – understanding how the Catalyst Stack of our past and the present situations affect our reactions, and responses, leading to the creation of new beliefs, habits, behaviours and responses/

The BE elements and the RAMP-IT framework, uncovering how they intertwine to create a holistic approach to personal growth and emotional resilience.

By understanding and integrating Safety, Gain and Loss, Clarity and Confusion, and Self and Ego, we've learned to navigate life's challenges with greater calm and presence. Applying the RAMP-IT factors —Purposeful, Mind/Body State, Accountable, Resourceful, Influential, and True—has empowered us to set meaningful goals, manage stress, and build fulfilling relationships.

THE ONGOING PROCESS OF TRANSFORMATION

Transformation is not a one-time event but an ongoing process.

The most important thing you can do today is start using what is in this book consciously. It takes practise. It takes time. It takes getting it wrong and not knowing why you are triggered or emotional, other than knowing you don't have a solution to process the situation calmly, yet.

As you continue to practise the principles of BE-ing and self-coaching, you refine your ability to respond rather than react to life's situations. You grow more adept at creating supportive environments, setting clear intentions, and maintaining emotional balance. Each step forward, each moment of reflection, and each application of these principles bring you closer to your true self and enhances your capacity for joy, resilience, and fulfilment.

NEXT STEPS AND CONTINUED GROWTH

This book contains enough information to keep you going for a while and help you start figuring out how to apply it to the many diverse and ever-changing situations you'll find yourself in.

However, this book is like learning to drive: It shows you the basics of getting on the road. However, if you want to go off-road or start Formula One racing, you need different resources and help.

That's where the following options come in if you're interested in learning more, and getting help implementing it all faster.

1. **Get the RAMPIT RUNDOWN Books**: To deepen your understanding and expand your practise, consider exploring other books in this series. Each book covers specific aspects of BE-ing, such as parenting, relationships, teenage life, driving, leadership, addictions, faith and more, each offering additional insights, tools, and exercises to support your journey. As they are completed, they will be available at https://nolancollins.com/rampit-rundown-ebooks as downloadable PDFs, along with workbooks, videos and contextual one-pagers for more specific situations within the scope of the book. They will also

be added to Amazon for paperback versions, and my goal is to get them in stores by mid-2025.

1. **Join the Community**: Engage with a community of like-minded individuals who are also on the path of BE-ing in the Self.Coach community. Sharing experiences, challenges, and successes with others can provide valuable support, inspiration, and accountability. Join online forums, attend workshops, and participate in community events to stay connected and motivated. You will get weekly training and access to every e-book, one-pager, video and course* I create for a low monthly fee, and that is for two people! Visit https://nolancollins.com/ramp-your-shift-the-community

1. **Get Mentoring**: I now offer a mentoring program to guide you in your personal and professional growth. Mentoring provides personalised support, helping you navigate specific challenges and achieve your goals more effectively. The programs I offer combine training for the BE Elements and RAMPIT Framework, combined with mentoring (because I've been there too so can speak from experience!) and coaching to help you find the answers that fit your life, situation and environment). https://nolancollins.com/coaching-emotional-regulation

1. **Corporate Training**: Consider bringing the principles of BE-ing and self-coaching into your workplace. Corporate training programs can help create a more supportive, productive, and emotionally intelligent work environment. By fostering the principles of the BE Elements and RAMPIT Framework within teams and organisations, you can enhance collaboration, reduce stress, and drive success. I stress the importance of everyone in the company having the same training so offer both in-person training and online access to

whole companies. Contact me via https://nolancollins.com for details.

*Some courses are paired with mentoring / coaching and offered as separate programs.

The journey of BE-ing is a continuous, transformative process. By integrating the BE elements and RAMP-IT factors into your daily life, you can achieve greater emotional regulation, purpose, and fulfilment. Embrace the ongoing nature of this journey, and take advantage of the resources and community available to you for continued growth and support. Remember, each step you take brings you closer to living a life of true BE-ing.

ABOUT THE AUTHOR

Hello. I'm Nolan, the guy with a bit of an unusual mix on my resume—from orchestrating servers in fine-dining restaurants to teaching the gentle art of massage, from gliding across ballroom floors to navigating the ever-changing world of digital marketing, and of course, coaching people like us to find our own patterns in life's ever-changing kaleidoscope of shifts and challenges.

You could say my hidden talent is for spotting patterns, which turns out to be really handy. It's like having a shortcut to learning and teaching just about anything. Like the time I taught my kids to ride a bike using a dancer's frame — and they had it down in minutes. Or when I tweaked training systems in restaurants to get the staff more excited, less stressed, working more efficiently and boosting both profits and smiles.

Then there's the RAMP-IT Frame™ for Self-Coaching, and now, the four BE Elements™ you're about to dive into (The BE-4)., or, hopefully, already have. It's all about simplifying the complex, finding actionable nuggets that get you going, and laying down a rock-solid foundation so you can confidently build your house of cards... with glue!

I remember one time in North Carolina — I entered an amateur Country two-step dance contest. A friend of mine advised, "Stick to the basics and do them well." Well, we nabbed second place, outshining over twenty fancier, flashier dancers. That moment really drove home the power of knowing the basics for me.

There's also my dog, Saxon. He's my fluffy buddy for walking through the countryside near Cambridge, UK. Now, my kids—they're a whole other adventure. They've given me countless chances to level up my parenting game and just be a better guy all around. They're the gift that keeps on giving!

Post-divorce as the Covid lockdown ended, I gave myself permission to just be present. To be open. And surprisingly, I found bits of myself I'd misplaced along the way. Also, thanks to my amazing partner, who's been my relentless challenger and supporter. I was lost, but now I'm found — and yes, that line makes more sense to me now. The more work I do on myself, the more I discover bits of me that make life richer — being present, being happy, being loved, and just being more me for myself and all the people in my life.

So, here's to you finding your way to just... be... too.

Thank you for getting and reading this book. I sincerely hope you gained at least one thing that made sense, and creates a calmer, safer, more connected you in more situations.

instagram.com/rampitnolan

Printed in Great Britain
by Amazon

47417310R00129